OPPOSITIONAL DEFIANT DISORDER

Table of Contents

Introduction

Negative, aggressive, and defiant behavior toward authority people such as parents or teachers is a sort of disruptive behavior. The symptoms usually start in childhood but can carry on into adulthood. People with ODD might often be angry, lose their temper easily, argue with teachers and authority figures, or have problems taking turns in games. They might disobey rules, deliberately annoy people, or refuse to play by the rules of a game. Children with ODD are often unhappy with their schools and teachers and may have trouble adjusting to changes in their surroundings. There might be a pattern of rebellious behavior such as truancy, getting into fights, running away from home, or being uncooperative and difficult at school rather than direct disobedience to authority figures. They might have problems with behavior such as lying, stealing, bullying people, or vandalizing things that usually do not involve violence. Children and teenagers with ODD can also experience problems such as low self-esteem, lack of motivation in school, or feeling bored in their activities such as sports or hobbies. In young children, the symptoms are likely to include separation anxiety, temper tantrums, and bedwetting. The behavior might be ignored or criticized by parents or teachers, leading to the children's anger and hostility.Children with ODD are at a higher risk of being involved in other types of offending such as bullying or truancy,

as well as getting into trouble with the police or with the law. They might also have problems at school such as low grades or poor attendance. The symptoms of ODD can interfere with their ability to function socially and this leads to social isolation and withdrawal. Some children experience feelings of shame and embarrassment that they can be judged negatively by others due to their behavior. Children with ODD might have other disorders such as attention deficit hyperactivity disorder, anxiety, and depression. In adulthood, there is also a higher risk of acquiring antisocial personality disorder.

Children who have ODD are usually treated by a psychiatrist or psychologist. The treatment involves helping the child control their anger and improve their social skills by learning behavioral techniques when dealing with stressful situations. These techniques can include positive reinforcement for good behavior such as rewards for staying at home without getting into trouble, or positive feedback for completing tasks and achieving goals. The parents are also taught to reward good behavior and create schedules to help the child schedule their time effectively throughout the day, including homework time and time to rest. These behavioral techniques are used along with the use of medication to treat ODD in some cases. Children with ODD are also taught problem-solving techniques and self-help skills to help improve their social relationships, school work, physical health, stress management, and organization. Through work with a psychologist or psychiatrist, children participating in these programs are taught how to calm themselves down when they are feeling angry, rather than letting this lead to worse behavior. The treatment lasts anything from six months to a year.   ODD is different from other disorders because it is characterized by behavior that includes anger towards others and rebellion against authority figures such as parents or teachers. ODD is often found in children who have other disruptive behavioral disorders such as conduct disorder and attention deficit hyperactivity disorder. Children with ODD usually display behaviors such as lying, stealing, bullying or vandalizing property, or not following rules of games that do not involve violence. These behaviors might lead to difficulties in school or problems with peers such as fighting.

One of the most important things to remember when trying to differentiate between ODD and ADHD is that they are two different disorders despite them having several similarities. The difference between the two is that ODD children are mainly angry and argumentative, while ADHD children may not be angry but show hyperactive behavior, tend to move around a lot, and are easily distracted by their surroundings.

Once you have completed reading, I invite you to leave a review on this book. This would mean so much to me as it would help the dissemination of this material; you know I have been working hard on this product, and I really hope you enjoy it!

Chapter 1. What Is ODD?

At first, you may think your child's rebellious behavior is normal when they are still young; after all, toddlers are notorious for behaving in demanding and challenging ways. However, as they get older, and this kind of behavior doesn't become less frequent, what are your first thoughts supposed to be? All children and teenagers exhibit acts of defiance, a disregard for rules and authority figures, and vindictiveness from time to time. More typically, children are prone to throw tantrums while teenagers tend to be snotty, irritable, and extremely moody. When this behavior becomes applicable to Oppositional Defiant Disorder, children and teens' behavior suddenly becomes excessive and destructive and is most likely causing havoc in the child's personal life or at school.

Before defining Oppositional Defiant Disorder, it is important to distinguish between Oppositional Defiant behavior, which is a behavior present in all teenagers and children, and when it starts to manifest as Oppositional Defiant Disorder or ODD. Oppositional Defiant Disorder (ODD) can be best described as a repetitive emotive pattern, and this pattern should have lasted for at least six months to indicate that it is not an acute emotional outburst or an emotional issue that the child or teen had to deal with that is not typically related with a chronic condition. It is also directed specifically at authority figures in the child or teen's lives, who can be their parents, a coach, or an educator. Normally, there is no aggression involved as this behavior would point to another issue named conduct disorder. ODD is typically verbal and not normally physical at all. There is a list of symptoms, apart from the fact that their exhibition should be continued for a period of six months or longer that a child needs to be associated with for a possible diagnosis. Another detail that sets an ODD child or teen apart from a child exhibiting normal behavior is that one cannot seem to satisfy the child or teen's dissatisfaction or disdain with authority, authority figures, and nothing seems to make them happy.

Children younger than five are known to exhibit these types of defiant and argumentative behavior fairly often or even most days; in an older child, it may manifest at the very least twice a week. The main objective is to try and identify a pattern of behavior that is more intense and indicates a frequency that seems abnormal and has a high-intensity level compared to the behavior of a typical child. A functional way to measure the level of intensity of the child or teen's behavior is by looking for areas in their lives where this behavior is causing damage or impairment. For example, this ongoing tendency from your child or teen to cause conflict and object to authority may possibly make things very difficult at home. It can also lead to a variety of issues in school, including poor academic performance, social alienation, and the loss of friends. It is not uncommon for children or teenagers with ODD to become socially marginalized in environments like school. Although there is an estimate that about 3% of children suffer from ODD, medical professionals add that there is a strong possibility that the number is actually higher due to the fact that there may be many children and teenagers who have not been diagnosed with the condition.

The Physiological Development

Research has been conducted on the neurological aspects of children and teenagers who are diagnosed with ODD, and although no hard evidence was found, an open question remains among specialists about some neurobiological differences between children diagnosed with ODD and those who are not. An interesting research-based observation postulates that ODD is more prevalent in boys than in girls, only prior to the onset of puberty. However, after the onset of puberty, the number of cases starts to even out between the sexes, with ODD affecting 9% of girls and 11% of boys. It is also said that the way symptoms are displayed is different between the sexes, which may be relevant to the general ways young girls and boys approach and handle different situations.

There are studies indicating that some factors can make specific children more susceptible or likely to develop ODD than others. One of these factors that play a role in how likely a child or teen is to develop ODD or other conduct disorders is a genetic component. An interesting link is made between individuals diagnosed with mood disorders, ADHD, antisocial personality, and substance abuse disorders, and the likelihood of a first-degree relative (children) developing ODD. These are the physiological and neurological components of ODD that have thus far been discovered, but also in existence is a strong nature versus nurture argument which postulates that the manifestation of ODD occurs due to an interplay between genes and the environment the child or teenager is in. There is some encouraging news in statistical data, though, as an estimated two-thirds of children diagnosed with ODD will be able to deal with and overcome their destructive symptoms and behavior, and when a child who is diagnosed with Oppositional Defiant Disorder reaches the age of 17, there is a 70% chance that this disorder will no longer be playing a dominating role in their life and that they will not be experiencing any symptoms of ODD.

Symptoms and Behavior

There are specific symptoms a parent should be on the lookout for if they suspect that their child or teenager may suffer from ODD. This list is quite extensive, but the child does not have to indicate signs of all the listed symptoms; as we previously mentioned, only four symptoms are required for a probable diagnosis. The symptoms on the list include situations where a child or teenager often loses their temper or is just as often annoyed and touchy for no apparent reason. These children also exhibit resentful attitudes and behavior and are often angry at authority figures or in situations where they have to follow rules.

ODD symptoms also include a hostile and argumentative attitude towards any figure they may deem to be an authority figure, and if an authority figure makes a request, the child or teen will not comply with such a request, especially if it's related to rules or adhering to rules. If your child or teen often goes out of their way to deliberately annoy others and doesn't want to take ownership of their mistakes, these are also possible symptoms. ODD children and teens are known for blaming others when they get into trouble or when they are the focus of a disciplinary process. Finally, behavior that a concerned parent can look out for is spiteful and vindictive behavior. These types of behaviors do not necessarily happen so often; however, if you have observed them within the past six months, you can include them as a valid behavioral symptom. This diagnostic guide is based on the American Psychiatric Association's Diagnostic and Statistical Manual of Mental Disorders (DSM-5). Parents need to keep in mind that ODD symptoms may vary from person to person, so if you know someone whose kid has ODD and they behave in a specific way, try not to use the child as your parameter; use the provided set of symptoms instead.

We are all different and when it comes to mental disorders, we may have the same issue but display the symptoms very differently. Especially in a case like this where a child or teen only requires four of the eight main symptoms for an initial consultation; this can cause different children with ODD's behavior to be very much the same but also different. When looking for these symptoms in your child, keep your child's personality and temperament in mind as well to ensure that you identify the symptoms authentically and contextually. Some cognitive symptoms that are very common with ODD include a child or teen's inability to speak before thinking, having a difficult time concentrating, and frequent bouts of frustration (Valley Behavioral Health System, 2017; Mayo Clinic, 2018).

Causes, Risk Factors, and Co-occurring Disorders

It is imperative to also discuss co-occurring disorders as these may be a precursor or an indication that a child may be more likely to develop ODD. The child themselves does not have to have one of these conditions but may have a closely-related family member that does. On the other hand, conditions or disorders that typically manifest later in life like bipolar disorder are more likely to happen to children or teens who show symptoms of ODD. It is important when evaluating a child or teen with ODD to also look for signs of other co-occurring disorders. These conditions include attention deficit hyperactivity disorder or ADHD, learning disabilities, depression, bipolar disorder as earlier mentioned, and anxiety disorders. If a coexisting condition can be identified and treated in tandem with the ODD symptoms, chances are that the treatment may be significantly more successful as these co-existing conditions often aggravate ODD in a child or teen as it causes even more difficulty, confusion, and frustration. There have also been cases with children and teens diagnosed with ODD progressing to developing conduct disorder, where the child would develop a pattern of violent and disruptive rebellious behavior. To understand ODD as a whole, one also needs to understand which other conditions a child or teen may have that can aggravate the symptoms.

Anxiety Disorder

Although experiencing anxiety is normal in a stressful situation, having anxiety disorder points to a situation where someone experiences this state of angst or fear to such a point that it becomes all-consuming and affects their well-being and their ability to live a normal life. A physiological anxiety response happens when your brain senses a threat and responds by releasing hormones that put your body in defense mode. Children and teens can experience anxiety at school if they have to prepare for a big test when they didn't do their homework and the teacher is busy checking everyone's work, if they are waiting for test results, or if they experience relationship insecurity with their friends.

They can also experience anxiety at home if there are conflict situations between parents or siblings, the living situation is not stable, or if there are significant financial problems. However, these are all, although serious, normal reasons for a child to be anxious. When someone has an anxiety disorder, they may go through the same situations, but their level of anxiety is so high that it becomes overwhelming to them. A child or teenager with an anxiety disorder lives in a perpetual state of fear and anxiety, which causes them to avoid engaging in normal activities like going to school, socializing with friends, avoiding situations where you need to go out in public because you don't want to face other people and limit your communication with others, even your family.

Due to extensive research on the topic of anxiety disorders, several different types have been identified that may apply to younger individuals who may also have ODD. Firstly, there is what is called Generalized Anxiety Disorder, which is basically described as an excessive and unrealistic feeling of worry for what would normally be perceived as a situation that would not require that level of worry. Next, there is panic disorder, which includes feelings of anxiety and excessive worry, but is also specifically characterized by sudden feelings of overwhelming fear and panic, which induces a panic attack. A person may experience palpitations, chest pain and difficulty breathing due to chest pain and break out in perspiration during a panic attack. They experience a very high level of fear that dislocates them from their immediate surroundings and reality. The severity of this experience may sometimes lead to the individual feeling like they are having a heart attack or that they cannot inhale enough oxygen, which causes a choking experience.

Social anxiety disorder, also known as social phobia, is when you spend a lot of time premeditating and then excessively worry about everyday social situations. For example, from a child or teen's perspective, they will likely create a social scenario that may happen at school, picture the worst social outcome for them that would probably lead to embarrassment or shame, and then obsessively worry about this. Separation anxiety is a sort of anxiety that most commonly affects children, but it can affect anyone. After one of a child's parents passes, especially when they are still young, they may develop separation anxiety due to the fear of losing their other parent or any other family member. Although there is some legitimacy in such fear, especially after losing someone close to you, there are also individuals who experience an irrational fear when someone they love leaves or is not in their direct sight or contact. Additionally, anxiety can also be caused by certain prescription medications, so if your child is on meds, consult your doctor to find out about the side effects of the drugs and whether it may be causing unnecessary anxiety that could be exacerbating a condition like ODD. Anxiety is not a monolithic concept or condition, so when you are looking for signs of heightened anxiety in your child's behavior, be sure to consider these different types, which may give you more insight (Lerche Davis, 2003).

Depressive Disorders

There are three major types of depressive disorders commonly diagnosed among children and teens, which include disruptive mood dysregulation disorder, major depressive disorder, and persistent depressive disorder or dysthymia. In general, the term depression is thrown around a lot and can be used to describe feelings or experiences that are not related to actual depressive disorders. Everyone, adults and youngsters alike, experience times when they feel down, which are most likely caused by events during their everyday life. When a person does not have a depressive condition, however, this sensation of feeling 'down' will go away, and it is not considered the person's usual state of mind. For example, the word depression or "feeling depressed" is often used to describe a person's discouragement that results from an acute event that caused disappointment or loss. Depressive disorders involve a pattern of low mood levels that are interlinked with feelings of worthlessness and self-loathing. Depression in children is believed to have the same cause as depression in adults, which is a significant loss or deprivation early on in life.

Children who suffer from depressive disorders may not be as able as adults to articulate their emotional experiences, but when observing their behavior, these children or teens will most likely show poor academic performance, attempts to withdraw from society, and can even act out in a delinquent manner. Children and teenagers who suffer from a depressive disorder will appear more irritable or aggressive than sad, which is an important difference between adult and childhood depression. The behavior of children and teenagers who suffer from depressive disorders can manifest as overactive, aggressive, and antisocial behavior.

Firstly, disruptive mood dysregulation disorder usually starts manifesting between the ages of 6 and 10 years in children and is categorized by disruptive behavior and persistent irritability. This specific type of depressive disorder is closely related to ODD as their behavioral symptoms are so similar. Disruptive mood dysregulation disorder is also linked with ADHD and anxiety. The diagnosis for this type of depressive disorder can be made after the age of 6 or before the age of 18. When a patient moves into adulthood, this condition may evolve into unipolar disorder, which involves depression without any manifestations of mania or anxiety disorder. Be advised never to attempt diagnosing your child with any condition without the support of a medical professional, but disruptive mood dysregulation disorder usually requires a combination of behaviors occurring simultaneously for 12 months without there being three months gone by where one behavior is missing.

This is something you can observe in a doctor's absence. These behaviors are, firstly, aggressive outbursts disproportionate to the relevant situation and that can manifest in verbal and physical expressions of rage (these will most likely occur, on average, 3 times a week), then the child will also exhibit temper-based outbursts that appear to be inconsistent with the level of cognitive and emotional development for their age, and appearing angry and irritable most of the time. It is also important that the child's outbursts should be observed in 2 of the 3 settings they find themselves in daily, which are at school, at home, or in the presence of their peers.

A major depressive disorder is more common after puberty, but it can occur at any age. This type of depressive disorder is different from disruptive mood dysregulation disorder as it is characterized by a discrete depressive episode lasting about two weeks. If the disorder is not treated, remission may occur within 6–12 months. Recurrence risks are higher in children and teens that have had severe episodes, who have experienced an episode at a younger age, and children who have had multiple depressive episodes. Signs of major depressive disorder can be identified if a child, firstly, feels sad or even tearful mostly every day for a period of two weeks, and secondly, if the child experiences a loss of interest in things they would normally enjoy doing, which can appear as an expression of high-level boredom.

Along with these two main indicators, you may also come across symptoms like insomnia or hypersomnia, weight changes, which are mostly recorded as decreased weight in children, fatigue, difficulty concentrating, possible recurrent thoughts about death or suicide, and feelings of worthlessness or feeling rejected or disapproved of. Even a child experiencing guilt that is contextually inappropriate can be an indicator. Major depressive disorder in older children of an adolescent age can have harrowing effects like academic decline, substance abuse, and suicidal tendencies. Major depression in younger children and teens can cause them to fall behind academically and lose out on developing crucial relationships with their peers.

Persistent depressive disorder or dysthymia can be identified as a persistently irritable or depressed mood that usually lasts most of the day, on most days for more than a 1-year period. The condition also includes at least two of the following behavioral symptoms: feelings of hopelessness, insomnia or hypersomnia, fatigue, difficulty concentrating, low self-esteem, and either a decreased appetite or overeating.

For all of these types of depressive disorders that may manifest in childhood and adolescence, a clinical diagnosis is necessary for confirmation purposes.

However, it is unavoidable to notice how much the symptoms from some of these types of depressive disorders, which are also regarded as possible co-occurring disorders, resemble symptoms of ODD. For example, most types indicate irritable behavior, and the first type we discussed, which is disruptive mood dysregulation disorder, lists symptoms such as aggression and behavior that can affect their social development. This may very well be why these disorders co-occur, and the potential influence and aggravating factors they may have on ODD needs to be explored so parents can have clarity on this topic. Let's first move on to another disorder that is mainly characterized to start showing symptoms in young adulthood, but has also been diagnosed and studied in children and teenagers (Coryell, 2020).

Bipolar Disorder

Bipolar disorder often starts as a major depressive disorder in children, and symptoms of bipolar disorder can start showing during mid-puberty through to the mid-twenties. Even while a form of depressive disorder is a precursor to bipolar disorder, it is crucial to note that not all children who are diagnosed with one will develop bipolar disorder. Bipolar disorder, although an important component as it is seen as a legitimate co-occurring disorder of ODD, is not at all common among children. Previous diagnoses of prepubescent children who showed unstable moods at an intense level were diagnosed with bipolar disorder, but this diagnosis has changed to disruptive mood dysregulation disorder due to the progression of the condition typically moving in the direction of a depressive disorder and not a subsequent, fully-blown bipolar disorder as the child gets older. The development of bipolar disorder may occur after puberty in the young adulthood of an individual who had ODD as a child and can be linked to ODD in this way.

Bipolar Disorder, from a behavioral or symptomatic perspective, is characterized by periods of mania, depression, and what can be perceived as a "normal mood." The requirement for diagnosis is that these states are constantly alternating and recurring and that they can last for weeks or months before transitioning to another state or mood. Treatment for Bipolar Disorder typically requires psychiatric drugs, but therapy is also recommended.

There is no concrete evidence about what causes bipolar disorder, but medical experts and researchers believe that there is definitely a genetic or hereditary component combined with the dysregulation of the neurotransmitter's norepinephrine and serotonin, and also a likely contributing factor to a stressful life event.

When an adolescent goes through a manic period or episode, they may appear very positive, or even hyperirritable, and these moods can also alternate during a manic phase. They tend to go into a productivity overdrive, and their speech is noticeably rapid and driven. Their sleep patterns will change as they will start sleeping less and an inflated self-esteem or a grandiose self-perception will be noticeable. Mania can reach the point of psychosis, where the adolescent may lose touch with reality and may say things like they are God, they have supreme knowledge that no one else has, and they will have a severely impaired sense of judgment that will lead to reckless and self-destructive behavior like casual sex, binge drinking, and even drug abuse. Because of the serious repercussions, a manic episode may have on an adolescent's life, monitoring the situation and seeking professional help is crucial. If your young child has ODD, you don't have to expect or fear a transition into bipolar disorder as they grow older; however, if you are aware of the prevalence of this disorder in relatives, you can help your child by conducting some preventive behavioral observation.

Intermittent Explosive Disorder

The intermittent explosive disorder is characterized by extreme and aggressive outbursts that can include impulsive, violent behavior, verbal outbursts, where the reaction does not fit the context of the situation at all. It is usually observed as a gross overreaction that is blown completely out of proportion to the situation it is linked with. In adults, examples of the intermittent explosive disorder include road rage, domestic abuse, attempting to throw or break objects in your proximity, or extreme temper tantrums. The condition is classified as chronic, and a child can show symptoms of this disorder for years, although the severity of the episodes or outbursts will decrease as the individual gets older.

The symptoms of the intermittent explosive disorder can be quite unsettling to someone who has never experienced an outburst like this before. A completely authentic episode can develop and erupt within the time span of 30 minutes, completely without warning. What makes this disorder trickier to diagnose is that these outbursts can be separated by weeks or even by months of non-violent and non-aggressive behavior, which can make it look like an isolated incident. It can also be the case that the main outbursts tend to be physically aggressive and that they are interval-led with verbal outbursts, which appear less serious. A person with intermittent explosive disorder can be chronically angry, irritated, and generally impulsive.

An outburst or episode can be either accompanied or preceded (or both) by a tight feeling in one's chest, tremors and palpitations, a tingling feeling under the skin, a sudden surge of energy, racing thoughts, and rage or irritability. Have any of these symptoms ever occurred in your child? Verbal and physical outbursts are usually accompanied by shouting, temper tantrums, heated arguments, the shoving or slapping of others, vandalism or causing property damage, and threats to harm people or animals. After the episode or outburst is over, the child or individual may experience a sense of relief, and they will feel physically tired. At a later stage, they will experience shame, remorse, guilt, regret, or embarrassment.

There are multiple causes of intermittent explosive disorder, and they can act on each other. This means that the disorder seldomly has a singular cause. The first component that can cause the intermittent explosive disorder is, as with most disorders, genetics. Genetics are not often ruled out as a causal factor when it comes to mental disorders, and if there is a family member, specifically a direct family member who has also shown symptoms or received a diagnosis for this specific disorder, this is a valid reason to keep your eyes peeled. The other frequently present contributing factor is the environment. As environmental factors cannot ever be ruled out entirely when looking at the cause of mental illness, they will also remain a potential causal component. However, there are specific environmental circumstances that are isolated and emphasized in this case, which include physical and verbal abuse.

Exposure to this type of harmful behavior at a young age can trigger the intermittent explosive disorder. Finally, a child can develop intermittent explosive disorder due to differences in brain function, brain chemistry, and brain structure. This statement is only based on observations and, although the idea is completely conceivable, concrete evidence has yet to be produced. Finally, two risk factors that link with these causes provide a reason to keep you alert as a parent of this disorder. They are, firstly, if the child has suffered physical abuse, and secondly if the child has been diagnosed or shows signs of other mental disorders.

Children with intermittent explosive disorder will ultimately struggle to form meaningful relationships, they will experience inconsistencies and trouble with their mood and, as a consequence, they will experience difficulties at school and at home. If the condition is untreated, they may resort to self-harm, and they can develop other health issues such as diabetes, heart problems, high blood pressure, and experience physical pain (Mayo Clinic, 2020).

Intellectual Developmental Disorder

Intellectual developmental disorder, also known as IDD, is more of a newly discovered and labeled as a neuro-developmental disorder where the symptoms and characteristics were previously placed under the same umbrella as what was then called "mental retardation." However, IDD is not a full manifestation of mental disability, so the disorder was given its own identity and is now identified as a mental disorder.

The key components of the intellectual developmental disorder are linked to a child having certain developmental deficits or shortcomings when it comes to specific intellectual processes and intellectual functioning. These functions include proper reasoning, effective judgment, planning, abstract thinking, and they can have difficulty with learning in general.

A child with IDD's learning processes is remarkably slower than a child who is considered to have no impairments in this regard. The signs or symptoms of this disorder can be observed in multiple stages of a child's development. For example, children with IDD may have trouble starting crawling and standing up, and they may only do this successfully much later than other children. Their vocal abilities are also likely to develop later, and as they become old enough to go to school, problems may occur in the classroom as they tend to struggle with clear communication and will find it difficult to interpret and apply new information that is presented to them.

A child with IDD will struggle to keep up with their peers in school due to the slower processing of information and their inability to understand some concepts. They will, for example, not have the ability to develop problem-solving skills, they can indicate a lack of social inhibitions or an understanding of how social norms work. In this case, though, they do so because they do not understand social boundaries as opposed to a rebellious child purposefully crossing social boundaries. A child that has IDD can struggle with everyday tasks that other children will see as completely normal, like giving someone the correct change, following cooking instructions, or organizing the items in the pantry.

The risk factors for IDD include genes or genetic syndromes, malformations occurring in the brain of the child, the influence of drugs or alcohol during pregnancy, traumatic brain injury, complications during labor, types of seizure disorders, and even severe social deprivation. The diagnosis for IDD includes an IQ test, where a score below 70 can be an indication that the child may have IDD. However, this IQ score is not enough for a comprehensive diagnosis; the child needs to be observed to see if there are other adaptive or communication issues present. It is assumed that this disorder is already present before birth, except if the child suffers physical trauma or a toxic exposure before, they reach the age of 18 (Child Mind Institute, 2020a).

Language Disorder

Children who have language disorders generally struggle with both understanding and speaking a language, usually their native language. Language disorder is not the same as speech sound disorder; however, the two can be confused. Speech sound disorder concerns problematic sound production.

Language disorder can be described as a communication disorder where a child experiences constant issues with language use, as well as language acquisition. For example, a child can struggle to process specific linguistic information like sentence structure, vocabulary, and discourse. The disorder affects a child's ability to process and produce language and also forms of communication, may they be spoken, written, or even gestural. Children with language disorders do not, however, have any trouble producing speech sounds.

If your child has a language disorder, symptoms have most likely manifested from a very early stage in their childhood; however, you will only realize this later when their functioning requires more complex linguistic processing. A child that has a language disorder will usually have issues with comprehending and processing what other people say, especially compared to the speed of comprehension of a child that does not have a language disorder. This disorder can cause the child to leave out words from a sentence when speaking, use placeholders like 'um' a lot while they search for words when speaking, and tend to repeat or echo parts of questions, whole questions, and use incorrect tenses often. These children appear shy as they are reluctant to talk because it is a difficult process for them.

If you have a history of language disorders in your family or ancestors, this may be a cause to be on the lookout for signs and symptoms. A diagnosis requires a child to have problems or deficits in communication that is deemed appropriate for their age, affecting their vocabulary, sentence structure, and if they have trouble using the correct language to transfer information in a conversation. The most effective treatment for language disorder is speech therapy and can be accompanied by cognitive behavior therapy and psychotherapy (Child Mind Institute, 2020b).

Conduct Disorder

Conduct disorder is often mistaken for the oppositional defiant disorder. However, if one looks at the symptoms, there are some surprising differences that will have you wondering why you compared them in the first place. Nonetheless, it's best to know what conduct disorder is as this will help you understand the symptoms of your child's ODD. Here's a rundown of the most frequent conduct disorder symptoms, inclinations, and actions in kids.

Conduct disorder or the prevalence thereof affects about 10% of children, and the symptoms most commonly start to show in late childhood to early adolescence. This disorder is also more common in boys than in girls, and it is different from the oppositional defiant disorder due to its significantly higher level of violent behavior. The definition of conduct disorder is a pattern, described as persistent or recurrent, of behavior that violates the rights of other individuals and also violates age-appropriate societal norms or rules.

Although genetics is not ruled out as a causal factor for this disorder, a heavy emphasis is placed on the child's home environment, and if a child's parents regularly participate in substance abuse or have been diagnosed with disorders like schizophrenia, ADHD, mood disorders, or an antisocial personality disorder, this can be a strong indicator to the cause of conduct disorder development. This being said, it is not completely uncommon for a child growing up in what would be perceived as a healthy and high-functioning household to develop conduct disorder. So, what makes conduct disorder different from oppositional defiant disorder or ODD? Here are some signs to look for, though I don't think you'd have to look very hard.

A child with conduct disorder doesn't have the ability to empathize with others in terms of their well-being and emotions, and they can easily interpret another child or adult's behavior as intentionally threatening even if there are no indications of a threat whatsoever. Children with conduct disorder want to cause damage and do so by acting aggressively, bullying others, conducting acts of physical cruelty on others, displaying and using weapons, forcing another into taking part in a sexual act, and they have no feelings of regret or remorse for their actions. They will likely divert their aggression and cruelty toward animals, and they have no issue lying, stealing, or vandalizing property. They do not tolerate rules and are likely to run away from home or stay away from school.

Although boys are more likely to have conduct disorder than girls, there is still a notable difference in their symptoms which can be valuable knowledge to have. On the one hand, boys are more likely to vandalize, steal, and fight, which points to more physical conduct issues. On the other hand, girls are prone to run away from home, tell lies, and get involved in prostitution. Both sexes are likely to use illicit drugs and can have suicidal tendencies. It is crucial for any suicidal tendencies or suicide attempts to be taken very seriously in these cases (Elia, 2019).

Complications

There are serious effects from undiagnosed and untreated ODD that can cause permanent damage to your child's life. Early detection, although not always possible because of the six-month time span required for the detection of any legitimate initial signs, is crucial for the well-being of the child or teen because, as the condition becomes more severe, it will lead to serious complications in their lives that can last until adulthood. These complications include social issues like a loss or a complete lack of friendships and close relationships, the subsequent inability to develop any sort of meaningful relationships, they can go through life experiencing social isolation, and while they attend an educational institution, this setting will most likely be difficult for them to adjust to and to function in.

If ODD goes on untreated and the child or teen transitions into adulthood, issues may persist and even show further development. For example, such an individual would indicate an ongoing pattern of broken relationships and relationship conflicts, they would typically try to control those around them, which is one of the causes of their social alienation and isolation. Another is undeniably an individual's inability to let go of a grudge or being unable to forgive someone, which can also completely destroy a relationship. And then, when these defiant little ones grow up, they still don't deal well with authority figures, and this time, it may cost them their jobs or they may end up in a jail cell (Valley Behavioral Health System, 2017; Mayo Clinic, 2018).

How to Process this Information Overload

This chapter has provided a myriad of information about mental disorders, starting with the main topic of discussion, which is oppositional defiant disorder, and then moving on to a lengthy discussion of potential co-occurring conditions or disorders that are or have been associated with ODD. So, what do we as concerned parents need to make of all this information? Some of the symptoms discussed in a few of the co-occurring conditions like mood disorders and intermittent explosive disorder can seem downright frightening, and they can make you fear for your child's health and sanity. However, the purpose of the first chapter is to lay all the facts about ODD bare so the rest of the guide can continue based on information. This chapter is synonymous with the mantra "knowledge is power" and aims to arm you with the most up-to-date information out there that may help you and your child.

There is one golden rule when going through these details, especially from a parent's perspective. We know how protective we are of our children. Don't mix knowledge or information with emotion, or worse, paranoia or neuroticism. Chapter 1 is your toolbox where you can read up on and find information about different components that may contribute to your child's condition. Yet, it is extremely important that you don't diagnose your child yourself based on this information; if you know that your child has ODD but you suspect that there may be another disorder lurking in the background, the best thing you can do for your child is taking them to a therapist or psychiatrist and tell the medical professional about your observations. Feel empowered by everything you've read so far. In the next chapter, we're focusing on you, your power as a human being, and how you can manifest your strength in a way that will benefit your whole family.

At What Age Can Oppositional Defiant Disorder Be Diagnosed?

The diagnosis of ODD is not made with ease, as the condition often overlaps with other developmental disorders or mental health issues. Thus, it can be difficult to establish which manifestations are exclusively caused by the oppositional defiant disorder.

As a general rule, the earliest a diagnosis of oppositional defiant disorder could be made is around the age of four. Up to the age of three, it is part of normal development for children to exhibit oppositional and defiant behaviors. They are seeking independence, discovering the power of saying "no," and testing the limits of parents, caregivers, or educators.

It falls to an experienced child psychiatrist or developmental psychologist to determine whether the behavior of a child is age-appropriate or extreme. For the diagnosis of ODD to be made, one must demonstrate a recurrent behavioral pattern for at least six months, including an angry or irritable mood, argumentative or defiant behavior, and vindictiveness. The behavior must involve at least one other person, including those outside the family.

Children of a young age, usually under three, often have temper tantrums. These resemble some of the manifestations of the oppositional defiant disorder, and this is the reason the diagnosis process is often delayed. One must remember that these tantrums are age-appropriate behavior and should not be interpreted as ODD.

In the majority of the cases, the condition is diagnosed upon finishing pre-school or when the child is just starting elementary school. Mental health professionals will perform a comprehensive evaluation to make an accurate diagnosis. They will take into account the fact that the condition appears simultaneously with other behavioral issues, seeking to make the distinction between the associated manifestations.

What Does the Evaluation Entail?

The assessment will consider the overall health of the child, with special attention being given to the manifestations suggestive of ODD (frequency, intensity, and timeframe). The specialist will inquire about the way the child behaves in different settings, including at home, school, or when interacting with peers. A detailed history of the child's behavior in various settings can be useful for making an accurate diagnosis.

Family relationships will be explored during the evaluation as the family environment can contribute to the appearance of such issues. The healthcare professional will make detailed notes on family situations, discussing strategies that have been used to manage the child's behavior. They might also discuss less helpful strategies and inquire about other mental health issues. Special tests might be needed for children who suffer from learning or communication disorders.

When making the diagnosis, the specialist will want to talk not only with the child and his/her parents but also with other caregivers and teachers. It is important to explore every aspect of the child's behavior. Observing the child might be necessary and assessment tools are often employed for the testing one's mental health.

If there is the suspicion that the child suffers from an underlying health condition, the psychiatrist might recommend additional investigations. Both imaging studies and blood tests can be used to diagnose underlying medical issues that may be contributing to the behavioral problem. The investigations can be useful in excluding potential causes, such as drug abuse or mental health problems.

Depending on the age of the child, direct interviews might take place. However, children are rarely capable of explaining why they behave in a certain way, especially at a younger age. They may also not understand their symptoms, with parents and caregivers being more suited to talk to. Long interviews should thus be conducted with all of the adults involved in the child's upbringing.

When Should a Diagnosis Be Sought?

One might consider getting the child evaluated for ODD if the behavioral problems, suggestive of this diagnosis, persist for over six months. A diagnosis must be sought if family dynamics are affected by the child's behavior, with other children and parents experiencing significant distress. The same is true in cases where the child's educational performance is harmed or their social relationships are restricted. If the child cannot learn, has trouble maintaining friendships, or is at risk of harm, ODD might be the problem.

Tests and Tools Used for the Diagnosis

The American Psychiatric Association produced and published the Diagnostic and Statistical Manual of Mental Disorders (DSM-5), which provides precise diagnostic criteria for oppositional defiant disorder in children. Based on these criteria, the condition can range from mild to severe. The checklist in the DSM should always be compared to the behavior of the child, including direct answers from him/her (if old enough). The Anxiety Disorder Interview Schedule is a structured interview in which both the parent and the child answer questions regarding such mental health issues. The specialist might also resort to the Eyberg Child Behavior Inventory, which is completed by the parent and assesses the behavior of the child. Another potential tool used for diagnosis is the Child Behavior Checklist, which is also filled in by the parent and contains specific sections that can be used for the assessment of suspected oppositional defiant disorder. Last, but not least, the Parental Stress Index can be used to determine how stressed the parent is, following the child and his/her behavior, other adults, and life events.

The earlier the diagnosis is made, the sooner an intervention plan can be created and the child's behavior improved. Parents who suspect that their children might suffer from ODD should not delay going to a specialist as only a trained professional can make an accurate diagnosis and recommend the most effective intervention strategies.

Chapter 2. Guide for Parents with a Child with ODD

If your child has ODD and you are having a tough time dealing with them, there are many things you can do to help. One thing that is extremely important is to talk to your child about their behavior when they misbehave. Use a tone of voice that shows empathy for their actions and be sure to use language that allows for honest expression without blame. Explain the difference between acceptable and unacceptable behavior so that they know what is expected of them. Do not punish or shame them for past behaviors because this will only make the problem worse, but offer a consequence if it does happen in the future. If you get frustrated, you need to ask yourself what is going on in your life that has triggered the behavior, then go do something that takes you away from the situation. Try not to turn off your cell phone when home so it can give you time away from the situation.

DO:

Talk about the feelings and feelings of others. Explain that if he is hurt about something, he can talk to us about how he feels. It will be okay if he cries, just don't yell at him or punish him. This is how we know we are talking to each other and not fighting over who was most hurt by something.

Make sure he knows that we are there to listen to him and help him when he is hurt. Let him know you love him and that he is special.

Forget about your own feelings and stay in the moment, knowing that things will turn out okay. It is okay for us to feel angry or upset, but it is not okay for him to act out this anger with our kids in the house. It may seem like it feels good when your child does this, but it is not okay in our household because we believe children should do their best to behave respectfully and use good manners at all times! We will never allow inappropriate behavior within our home. It is okay to feel hurt, but it is not okay to hurt others.

If you are angry with your child because of his behavior, tell him that you are upset because of his behavior. Do not say you're upset because he doesn't act like his brother or sister, or because he's always so quiet. Make sure your kids understand that we love all of them equally and don't treat them differently just because we are upset about their behavior. If a parent says this in the heat of the moment, children may feel iffy about the family relationships and can take this confusion out on each other at a later time.

If you feel like you cannot control your child's behavior, it is not your fault. It is because he doesn't want to be in a respectful and calm state of mind. You can make your child's life really difficult by making sure you're always on top of him about what he can do and how he should act. Children will take out their frustration on each other when they feel as if they are being watched or controlled too much by their parents. This will cause resentment among siblings (and even children of other parents!) that could last well into adulthood if not addressed immediately.

If you are upset, do not yell at your child. This will teach him that there is something wrong with him if you get angry at him. Shouting is not fair to those around you and is never a good way to treat a child. When they hear their name called or see the look of anger on your face, they may feel that yelling is the only way to get things done.

If you're constantly upset and yelling at them, children may not understand that you're upset about something else. They may think you don't want to talk about their behavior. When they hear you yell and fight with each other, they may get frustrated and take it out on their siblings. This can have a cascading effect, with youngsters failing to learn proper behavior because no one is providing a good example for them.

If you go through a bad day, it won't mean that your child will start acting out at home or school. We can't let our bad days interfere with how we treat our children. When a parent has a difficult day at work and takes it out on their child at home, the child may cause problems at school. It is not fair to your kids to treat them this way.

If you need a time-out, allow your child to be alone in his room while you do this. Let him know you will be back when you feel better so he knows it doesn't mean forever. He needs to see that time-outs are only used when someone is upset and needs a break from the situation. When your child is yelling at you, do not respond. If you do, this will teach him that he can get a reaction out of you when he is upset. This will cause other issues in your home because the children will know how to make you upset by that behavior. Once your child knows his actions affect your emotions, it can be very hard to correct them without being angry with him again.

If you take a dip in personality and become rude or cold with them, try not to use anger as a way of dealing with their behavior. That'll only make the situation worse for everyone and could result in harsh feelings between family members for years to come. Don't yell at or humiliate them.

Be consistent, fair, and predictable. If a parent gives a consequence but then backs down when they are angry and forgives their child, the child will know he can get away with bad behavior. Be sure your kids know that you will follow through on consequences because this is the only way for them to learn how to behave properly in different situations.

If you set boundaries for your child, let him know why those rules are in place so he understands where his limits are and who is responsible for enforcing them.

If you set a boundary but your child ignores it, be sure to let him know that he disobeyed the rule by not listening to you and this is what will happen if he continues to ignore these rules.

Be aware of your own feelings and how they may affect your child's behavior. We can't control what our children do or how their actions make us feel, but we can control the way we react to their actions. If you get angry with them and yell at them, they won't understand that you are truly upset about something else (like their behavior) and will feel like they are winning when they see that you're upset. The same goes for being cold and ignoring them. They will think you are mad at them for no good reason and may act out because of that.

Take time to understand when your child is being challenged in your home so you don't take it out on him with your own behavior. If you get frustrated with him, you must learn to direct the anger away from him before it gets the best of you! The anger and frustration that is directed toward children can cause feelings of hopelessness and helplessness for them, causing even more problems in their lives.

If your child is acting out or displaying bad behaviors or discipline techniques, it's important to examine what makes up these behaviors. Your child may be trying to manipulate you because he doesn't want to do things the way that you want him to or follow the rules that you have set for him. He may know very well that these behaviors are not acceptable and he knows you will get upset if he continues. The more adverse reactions you show, the more likely it is that your child will continue this behavior in hopes of getting something different out of you. This is when children will test limits and boundaries in their home because they'll feel as if they are getting away with something by having their parents behave this way.

28

Let your child know how much respect, love, and trust he has in your family and what type of behavior makes his family happy. Teach them to show respect and gratitude towards their family by respecting themselves, others, and the world around them.

If they act out, use a time-out when they are not listening and still acting out. If you need to tell him that he is acting out, he'll know this is a serious situation. If he continues to act out, take him to the room where he can be alone or with the child who has called the time-out. This will teach him that there are consequences if he refuses to listen and obey you. Having just one parent in an argument with another really sends a bad message that parents are not in control of themselves as well as their children's behavior.

If you feel like you are losing control of your children, have a conversation with your spouse and/or any other adults in the family to get some things in order before you lose it and start yelling at your children. The more you yell at them, the worse they will behave when they are around you. If your family is having trouble with discipline, talk to other parents about their experiences so that you might benefit from them as well.

Be aware of how others treat your children when they act up or misbehave. It won't have the same effect on your children when the others around them treat their behavior with respect and kindness.

Set some limits for your child so that he knows what will happen if he doesn't follow them. You don't want to teach him that he can make you angry just by acting up, but you want to teach him that there are consequences when he doesn't behave properly in his home. When you set a limit and stick to it, explain why this is occurring and what behavior you anticipate him to exhibit instead of what you don't. This will help him learn how to understand limits in his life while also teaching him that there is a way to behave correctly without being punished.

Use positive reinforcement for good behavior. Be sure to reward your child for good behavior or the times when he is not acting out or misbehaving. This will help him understand that being a good person and doing the right thing is much better than not getting what he wants (or what he doesn't want). He'll also try to act out so you'll give him attention, but if you're giving him positive attention without having to act out, he won't feel as though he has to draw your attention with bad behavior.

If your child is struggling with his emotions or feeling depressed, be sure to seek help from a medical professional. This could be an indication of something more serious, and your child's doctor may need to prescribe medication.

If your child is acting out because he doesn't like being in a certain situation, he'll make it difficult for you to have him where you don't want him. He'll act out and refuse to go where you want him, so think about how much trouble you're going to have if this continues or how tired it will make you when he does this. If the situation is that bad for you, perhaps there are other ways for your family to get things done so that the family can spend time together at the park or something else fun.

Think about the times when you have acted out and think about your parents' reactions to your actions. Were they angry with you? Did it help you learn how to behave or did it make you want to act out more in hopes of getting something different? If your parent's behavior didn't do any good, don't do what they did! Think about what was considered respectful behavior back then and try to apply that so that your child understands that this is how he should behave.

Be sure that you are prepared to handle bad behavior if they take a turn for the worse. Because there is a certain amount of unpredictability, be sure that you know what all of the important information is just in case anything goes wrong.

Children will be children. If you have never dealt with these types of situations before, you may end up simply reacting to their bad behavior, which they may learn how to get out of the situation by repeating it enough times to receive a reward. Remember that you want to teach them how to act appropriately, not how they can try and use your reaction against you so they can get what they want. If this is an issue between you and your child, find a way for him to understand what kind of behavior is acceptable and do not let him act out in order to receive attention from you if he doesn't like something.

Children can sometimes be very stubborn, but if you have a sense of humor and show them that you are not upset with them, they may respond to your behavior instead of their own reaction to the situation. Just make sure that you won't be giving them too much attention when they misbehave or they won't learn how to behave properly.

If there is a problem in your family and it is affecting your children's behavior, talk to other parents about what you can do so that you have an understanding of what type of behavior will work for your family. Do not use each other as free babysitters when the children are misbehaving in their homes. The problem needs to be addressed and fixed as soon as possible.

If your family continues to have problems with your children misbehaving, be sure to set a plan of action on how you will handle the behavior. This will enable you to know exactly what to do in the event that something similar occurs, preventing you from panicking and acting out against your children.

It's important that your children be aware of how they are expected to behave in their home and outside of it so that they know what is expected from them before they are involved in an argument or situation with other people, or before they get into trouble at school or other places where there may be consequences for their actions.

Chapter 3. Peaceful Parents Raise Happy Children

Parenting is a task that requires a lot of responsibility. It is a life-long, full-time job that no parent should neglect and should perform to the best of their abilities.

It's likely to happen that sometimes parents cannot fulfill their duties for whatever reason. They are also human after all, so they could be mentally distressed and may neglect their duties. This is completely natural, but a child won't be able to understand this situation. If a parent behaves this way, the child will be deeply affected, as will their upbringing.

In such circumstances, the child may acquire a mental disease as an adult and be unable to live life to its full potential. Their personality could become severely warped, making the child depressed, stressed out, and dissatisfied. That is why it is of the utmost importance that parents understand their responsibility in not allowing this to happen to their children.

As a parent, you should try to keep a calm and peaceful attitude as you raise your children. In this section of the book, I'm going to talk about some of the tools that will help you in your role as a parent to handle your child's aggressive behavior while maintaining your inner peace.

Better Understanding

The development of a deeper understanding between you and your child is one of the most essential reasons why you should adopt a calm approach to raising your child. One of the major issues that both parents and children have to deal with is a lack of understanding of one another. The very obvious generation gap between you is the main thing to try to overcome. A parent may not be able to understand how the new generations, of which their child is a member, think and act right away. A parent may try to restrict a behavior that is perfectly normal for the child, or might not be able to understand the things their child talks about.

In the same way, a child of a new generation will probably never understand the mentality, standards, and molarity of their parents. Since they belong to older generations and thus have a more "old-school" approach to life, children will have difficulty understanding where their parents are coming from.

In this situation, if parents become impatient and try to impose their beliefs on their children, it is quite likely that the child will rebel and refuse to follow their parents' guidance.

That is why, when dealing with your child, it is critical that you remain as cool as possible. If you raise your children in a way that fosters peace, they will be more receptive to your point of view, and you will also be able to understand your child better.

Build Trust in Your Relationship

Another huge benefit of a peaceful approach to parenthood is the trust that will develop between you and your child. Trust is one of the most important aspects in any kind of relationship. Think of it this way. Would you blindly follow a person you don't fully trust?

The same goes for children. You are your child's first role model and source of rules and standards for coping with the world as a parent. If your child sees that you're always angry and stressed out, if you constantly yell at them and lose your temper around them, then your child will not be able to develop any kind of trust in you. They will prefer to stay away and not share their thoughts and feelings with you rather than speak their mind confidently.

In this case, a peaceful attitude is extremely beneficial. Your child will naturally come to trust you if you establish a safe place for them to communicate their problems with you and take the time to actually listen to what they have to say. They will know that no matter what they're going through, you, as their parent, will listen and understand. This kind of trust is probably the most important aspect of a parent-child relationship.

Solving Problems with Ease

Another benefit that comes from peaceful parenting is that you will be able to solve problems with ease. It is impossible to solve any kind of problem in a satisfactory way when we are upset, stressed out, or angry. Now imagine if your child comes to you for help while you're in that state of emotional turmoil. Would you be able to offer the best help you possibly can? The answer is probably not. If you force yourself into problem-solving mode while you're upset, it is much more likely that you will make the situation even worse for everyone involved, including you and your child. This will, in turn, affect your whole family dynamic.

On the other hand, if you strive for a peaceful and calm state of mind, you will be able to handle problems more easily. Your mind will be at peak performance and the solutions you offer to any adversity will be much more efficient.

Treasure Special Moments

Yet another perk of a peaceful mind is that you will be able to truly treasure all those special moments with your child. When we find ourselves in constant emotional turmoil, we often miss the special moments that make our life precious. This also goes for all those wonderful moments you could be sharing with your child. Imagine that your child comes to you with some great news about something that happened in school or with their friends, but you're having a pretty bad day yourself and you're in no mood for a noisy child, so you tell them to go to their room and leave you alone for a while. You will have missed out on a precious moment of your child's development and growth, as well as the chance to celebrate their victories with them. This is also something that will deeply wound your child.

Earn Respect

If your child sees that you always try to handle problems with a cool head and peaceful attitude, this will, in turn, increase the amount of respect your child has for you as the adult in their lives. Conversely, if you let your emotions get the better of you and constantly display aggressive behavior around your children, they will eventually want to stay away from the toxic environment of their home as much as possible.

While we are not perfect by any means, it is important that our children see us not as disrespectful and angry adults. Rather, parents should strive to be role models that their children respect and would proudly emulate when dealing with their own stressful situations. If your child sees that you remain calm under duress, that you tackle your problems head-on and sensibly, and, above all, that you still show love and affection for your family, they will, in turn, adopt this kind of behavior as adults.

How to Manage Your Anger?

As I have mentioned before, anger is a part of human nature. As such, it is impossible to avoid becoming angry, nor should you try to. There will always be situations that make us angry, just as there will always be situations that make us happy.

So, how can you become a parent that fosters peace and calm if you can't help getting angry sometimes? Controlling your fury is the best line of action in this situation. It's perfectly valid to be angry, it's perfectly valid to be furious, but regardless of the intensity of your anger, you should do your best to keep it from spilling over to your parenting and affecting your child.

Here are some strategies for controlling your rage and preventing it from influencing your children.

Think Before You Speak

The golden rule of anger management: think before you speak. We often say things we don't mean when we're caught up in our own anger. We end up saying all the wrong things and hurting other people.

It is also very common that we shift the blame onto other people when we're upset and fail to see how we may also be responsible for creating a bad situation.

That's why it's so important that we make a habit of thinking before we speak. Even taking as little as five deep breaths before responding can completely alter our state of mind. We will be able to see the situation more clearly, as well as become aware of the other person's point of view, which might be enough to defuse the situation.

Express Your Anger When You Are Calm

It is perfectly natural to want to express our anger the moment it is triggered, but this is not always the best approach. Blowing up at someone who made you angry can lead, again, to saying things you don't really mean, losing perspective of the situation, and damaging your relationship as a result.

This goes for your children too. If they do something that makes you angry and you immediately express that anger, you may end up blaming the child for all the wrong things, especially if the true reason for your anger is something else entirely, and your child was just the trigger. This not only hurts your child but teaches them that it's okay to act that way when they're angry.

Try, instead, to express your anger once you have calmed down. Practice the mindfulness exercises in previous chapters and only then, address the problem. You will surely see the situation in a different light and will have avoided escalating the situation into one where both you and your child would have ended up hurt by words spoken in anger.

Get Some Exercise

As previously said, exercise is an excellent technique to cope with tough emotions such as rage. Not only is it a diversion for your mind, but physical exertion can help you channel all that intense energy you feel when you're angry.

Try going out and getting a walk or a run, or taking your anger out on a punching bag if you have access to one. Simply performing any kind of physical activity that appeals to you will improve your mood, as long as you enjoy doing it. Once you're done with your workout, you can return to handling the problem.

Take a Time-out

Time-out isn't just for your kids! If the feelings of anger and frustration get to be too much, take a time-out yourself. Remove yourself from the problem for a while and perform any calming activities that you find enjoyable. Give yourself some time to think about the problem in your own timeframe, at your own pace. Once you've talked yourself down from the worst of your anger, you can leave your time-out and handle the problem.

Identify Possible Solutions

Finding a good answer to a situation that really irritates you is difficult since we can't think clearly while we're angry.

That's why it's best to try to come up with a solution only after you've calmed down a little. Instead of reacting to the problem, give the previous methods for calming yourself a try before trying to find a solution. Think about the possible outcomes of each solution you come up with and watch out for any course of action that you may be choosing as a result of your anger. Always choose the solution that best promotes peace in yourself, your child, and your household.

Stick With "I" Statement

Simply put, "I" statements are those that begin with the word "I." When arguing with someone else, you should always try to phrase your sentences in this way. Don't shift the blame onto the other person.

Compare these two sentences:

35

"You always leave the door open!"

And:

"I am upset because you always leave the door open."

While both sentences may be conveying a similar idea, they are in fact, quite different from one another. The first sentence is a complaint about something the other person is doing wrong according to you. In the second sentence though, you are communicating to the other person that you are upset without attacking them. According to several psychological studies, taking the time to phrase your sentences as "I" statements will help to reduce your anger.

Don't Hold a Grudge

Some people find it hard to let go of their anger when they feel someone has wronged them. The harder you hold on to a grudge, the harder it is to see things clearly and eventually find a solution to the problem. The grudge continues to fuel the anger until it becomes impossible to go about your day-to-day life without feeling consumed by those emotions.

If you work hard toward forgiving other people though, you will find yourself feeling lighter and much more relaxed in your everyday activities. This will also greatly improve your relationship with the people around you, including your children.

Use Humor to Release Tension

Laughter really is the best medicine when it comes to stressful situations.

Sometimes, it's tempting to let ourselves be swallowed by our negative emotions rather than put in the effort to get out of them. We will isolate ourselves and listen to sad songs when we're depressed, for example.

Next time you're under emotional duress, give humor a try. Watch a hilarious movie or TV show, look up amusing videos on YouTube (there are a lot!), or phone a friend with who you can joke around with. A good laugh is a perfect way to get you out of a rough emotional state and will give you a much-needed respite from the stress.

Practice Relaxation Techniques

I have talked about this in previous chapters, but relaxation techniques are always a great way to manage anger.

Aside from relaxation techniques, maybe you have a hobby that you haven't been able to indulge in since you became a parent. Try making some time to do things you truly enjoy doing, something that relaxes you and fills you with joy. Taking time for yourself is an important part of self-care and can greatly reduce stress, which in turn helps you to manage your anger much more easily.

If you don't have a hobby, try looking into things that interest you — this could be art, music, exercise, crafts, anything!

Know When to Seek Help

From time to time, we all require some assistance. The last thing you need is your anger damaging your personal, professional and social life, and potentially ruining your relationship with your children. If you find that your anger is too much to handle on your own, consider going to a professional. There's no shame in seeking assistance, and the benefits you'll receive will far outweigh any reservations you may have.

How to Stop Yelling at Your Child?

People who express their anger through yelling will sometimes blow up at a child who has angered them, even if they did so inadvertently.

The act of yelling at someone is never conductive to the resolution of the problem, but yelling at a child is even more problematic. Imagine, as before, a person three times taller than you, someone who is supposed to be looking out for you, is suddenly yelling at you for doing something you didn't even know was wrong. This can be extremely harmful to your youngster. It is hurtful and will likely result in them becoming people who yell at others to vent their frustrations.

If you are the type of person that yells when angry, here are some more ways you can control your anger before it gets to the point where you start telling at your child.

Know Your Triggers

The need to yell at someone is something that rarely, if ever, appears out of nowhere. In all likelihood, your anger has been building over a certain period of time — shorter for some people than others — and then something will happen that triggers this reaction. If you have a child with ODD, then your child is probably a recurring trigger for your anger and you will end up yelling at them before you know what's happening.

That is why it is critical to understand your triggers. Take a close at one incident where you lost your temper and yelled at your child. Examine the events leading up to the yelling and try to figure out what the trigger was. If you make it a habit of doing this, you will eventually be able to identify your triggers as they happen and stop yourself from yelling at your child before it happens. Over time and with patience, those triggers will lose their power over you and will no longer upset you to the point of yelling.

Give Kids a Warning

This works well when you already know your triggers. It's a good idea to give your child some warning about what behavior of theirs triggers your anger. If it's the kind of behavior that you wish to change, letting them know that it makes you angry can help in modifying it, which in turn prevents you from yelling at them.

If you're already angry and feel yourself about to start yelling, communicate your feelings of frustration to your child. If they're doing something that you don't wish to change in the long run, but rather just in that moment, tell them that what they are doing right now is making you uncomfortable or upset, and ask them to stop for a while.

Make a Yes List

A Yes List is a list of things that you will commit to doing before you start yelling at someone. Take a pen and paper and write down this list. It could be anything from going to the bathroom and taking some deep breaths, to jogging in place, anything that takes you out of the situation. Put that list somewhere visible, like the fridge or a mirror so that you can look at it whenever you feel like you're about to start yelling. Perform one or more of the items on the list if you feel your temper rising.

Teach the Lesson Later

Under normal circumstances, the best time to teach your child a lesson if they did something wrong is right after the fact. If you have a short fuse though, it's a better idea to wait to impart wisdom until after you've calmed down. If you lose your temper and yell at your child after they make a mistake, it's unlikely that you're really thinking about teaching them anything. You're probably just venting your anger and shifting blame onto your child.

In this case, it's better that you follow the previous techniques for defusing your anger and getting your child to stop the activity that is making you angry.

Once you've calmed down, it will be easier for you to communicate what bothered you about their behavior and for them to understand what you're trying to teach them.

Respecting your Child's Personality

In many ways, new generations are more advanced than their predecessors. Children today are fast-forwarding the evolution of humanity as a whole. We could see the knowledge accumulated over many generations in their comments if grownups took the time to listen to what they have to say and carefully answer their questions.

In particular, there is a certain tendency toward more emotional responses from children of newer generations than there was in the previous ones. Our parents (and their parents) would never have even dreamed of talking back to an authority figure at home or at school like children do today. Expressing emotions rather than keeping them bottled up is incredibly necessary for a child to grow into a balanced and happy adult. Letting our children do this and learning from them is the best way to move forward as a society.

It's not easy to overcome years (and generations) of repressed emotions. But if we look at our children, listen to what they have to say, and, particularly, try to identify what we find most annoying about their attitude; we will learn a valuable lesson about ourselves. If, for instance, you feel like your child doesn't show you your due respect, perhaps consider that you're not showing your child the same respect you want to receive. Many times, a certain behavior or attitude that annoys us about someone else, especially our children, is only a reflection of something that we dislike about ourselves.

Another example is when a parent tries to impose their way of doing things on their children. A child or teenager may already have their preferred way of doing something, but a parent insists they do it their way because "that's how things are done" or "because I said so." In an ODD child or a rebellious teenager, this will cause them to tell you to back off and mind your own business. Children and teenagers are also entitled to make their own decisions and if what they are doing isn't causing them or anyone else any harm, take a step back and let your child do their thing. It's important for you to remember that a child is not yours to control, but rather try to see the world through them and their experiences.

"Should I just give in and let my kids do anything they want?" I hear you asking. Well, yes and no. If what they want to do is not hurting them or the people around them or is illegal, then yes. Let your child do their thing, be who they want to be, and express themselves freely. A parent may not always like a certain aspect of their child's personality, but have to respect it nonetheless.

Let's say, for example, that Lily is a messy teen. She has the habit of always leaving her things all over the floor. Rather than getting angry and demanding that she pick up after herself, you could try asking her why she prefers to leave her things strewn about rather than picking them up. Does she feel safe and comfortable in a messy room rather than a clean one? If the answer is genuine "yes," then you can tell her that you're the opposite — that you don't feel comfortable in such an environment. Then you can try to reach a compromise. You can tell her that as long as she keeps the common areas in the house tidy, she can keep her room however she likes.

This will promote peace between you since you won't have a reason to be angry at the mess in her room and she will make the effort to be tidy in other areas of the house.

Your relationship with your child is bound to change once you open yourself up to the idea of learning about your child's personality and trying to accept the aspects of it that you don't really like. Do not be afraid of sharing these thoughts with your child! If they see you making an effort to meet them halfway, they will respond in kind. They will mature into people who are confident in their life choices and realize that they are free to be themselves.

If you find that your child shows little or no interest in exploring the world, cannot find a hobby and has no desire to be independent or autonomous, you should step in as their parent to offer help. The very first step is to reinforce your bond with your child, show them affection without them having to ask or fight for it. Let them feel relaxed in their relationship with you.

Here are some tips you can follow to help your child discover their hidden potential.

Tip No.1 — Give Your Child Affection

Hug your youngster and reassure him or her that you love them and will always look after them. This is especially important before parting when you send your child to school or to an unfamiliar place.

Be encouraging of your child's thoughts, ideas, and passions. Words like "it's amazing that you did this all by yourself!" are preferable to "I like what you did!"

Tip No.2 — Give Your Child Space to Self-Teach

Give your child a chance to try to understand the essence of things by themselves. Don't try to force them into early development. A child who has known the incredible feeling of discovering something by themselves will develop a self-sufficient personality later on. Unfortunately, most of today's children do not have the luxury to feel the excitement of a new discovery — the Internet already provides all the answers before they even know to ask the questions.

Make an effort to give your child opportunities to learn something new on their own, away from outside influences or expectations.

Tip No.3 — Give Your Child Time for Free Play

As mentioned before, your child needs time for free play, away from school, homework, and organized recreational activities. You have shown affection to your child and created a space for them to learn new things. Now it's time to just let your child do their own thing and for you to sit back and watch. How much time do they spend on an activity? How long do they think and plan before doing something — drawing, stacking blocks, dancing, etc.?

If your child gets bored too quickly, try not to be swayed into immediately playing with them. Some parents will bend over backward trying to keep their children entertained at all times. If you've already spent time playing with your child and feel like you need to step back, let them find ways to entertain themselves. Try telling them: "I'll be right here, I'm not going anywhere, but I can't play with you right now."

Tip No.4 — Give your child control and responsibilities

If you give your child a chance to steer the wheel and make their own decisions, they will slowly learn that they are in control of their life and will strive to realize their potential. Provide your child with an environment in which they are able to safely express their will. Give your child autonomy whenever possible. Ask them what they want to wear rather than picking out clothes for them. Let them decide what they want to have for breakfast or what time they want to go to bed. Trust that your child will make the right decisions for themselves and let them handle some responsibility — ask them to make lunch for the family or assign them some of the house chores.

Your role as a parent is to determine how much freedom to give your child and in what areas of their lives — where to relinquish some of your control, or all of it. It is up to you to decide when your child is ready to handle being in control and in charge of more responsibilities.

Chapter 4. Manage Their Stubborn Behavior

Growing teens find it hard to communicate freely with their parents. As a parent, you need to establish an open line of communication to avoid problems that may arise due to the aforementioned generation gaps. Keeping open and honest communication also ensures that your child does not develop aggressive behavior.

The link between a parent and their child is one of a kind. When they're little, children depend completely on their parents for care, security, and love. They naturally see their parents as their best friends, their protectors, and confidantes. They depend on their parents to love and support them without judgment, regardless of their mistakes and shortcomings.

As your child grows into a teenager, they may begin to exhibit aggressive behaviors. Their feelings become more complex and they suddenly find that they lack the words to communicate their thoughts and needs to their parents. This can lead to miscommunication and fights between you and your child.

Teenagers want to become adults, and they want to do it fast! This can be stressful for them as they are only just building their self-identity and learning to deal with the outside world. These are trying times for your child — they feel lost and vulnerable even though they try to put up a tough front.

It is a normal phenomenon that a teenager's mind becomes filled with confusion, conflict, doubts, anxiety, and other negative feelings. As your child goes through this tough time in their life, it is your responsibility as a parent to establish a channel of communication with them. Help them to put their thoughts and feelings into words, provide a safe space for them to do so, let them know that what they are going through is normal. Unless you create the right space at home for them to be able to express themselves, your teen will remain closed off and you will become a mere spectator in these difficult times.

In order to make parenting a teenager a little bit easier, try to curb your expectations. Try to accept your teen's passions (even if you do not fully understand them). Do not try to manage your teen, let them do their own thing. Try parenting courses and find things that both you and your teenager can enjoy doing together.

Adopting the Paradigms of Highly Effective Parents

If you want your child to develop a positive attitude, you have to first adopt the paradigms of highly effective parents, which can be summarized as follows:

Kids' Model of the World Is Different From That of the Parents

As a parent, the starting point is to change your mind in regards to your world model. You first need to understand and acknowledge that your view of the world is not the same as your child or teen's view. You shouldn't try to impose your views on them. What may seem to you like sage, worldly advice, may just seem like nagging to your teen and they may feel like you're trying to control them.

Parenting a teenager requires a lot of understanding, tolerance, humility, and patience. In some ways, this is probably the most challenging period you will face as a parent. Even so, parenting a teenager doesn't have to be a terrible experience. Here are some techniques you can apply to make parenting your teenager easier and more enjoyable for you.

Technique 1: How to Develop a Method to Raising Children

Some parents seem to be so successful in raising children to be responsible, caring, and honest adults, while many others just can't seem to get it right. First, it is important to realize that your responsibility as a parent is to help your children to develop a good, strong moral character. This is something that doesn't just magically happen; it takes a great deal of effort, time, and focus.

There are a number of parenting tips that will be very useful and valuable when it comes to helping your teen develop a strong character that will help them in the years to come. If you have a parenting partner, however, it won't matter how great these techniques are if you don't work together as a team.

Your partner should always be in your corner and you should always be in theirs. This requires that you establish communication and regularly discuss the values you want to instill in your children, as well as the best approach to achieve this. When it comes to discipline, love, and upbringing, team effort and constant communication will ensure that you and your partner are both on the same page.

When the going gets rough, as it inevitably will, sometimes having a few extra ideas up your sleeve can really make life a whole lot easier — for kids and parents alike. This is also something that requires full commitment from the parenting figures in the child's life. Here are a few more tips that have worked wonders for many parents.

Tip #1: Teach, Discuss, and Demonstrate Valuable Traits

As a parent, you must be a firm believer in discussing with your child what is appropriate behavior and what isn't. But just talking about it isn't enough. If you talk the talk, you've got to walk the walk, as the saying goes.

So, while it is important to talk to your child about the importance of being patient, for example, by explaining why we have to wait our turn at the grocery store or to go on a ride at an amusement park, it's equally important for you not to lose your cool when you're in a hurry and find yourself forced to wait as well.

Tip #2: Help Your Child Learn Responsibility

Chores are a must when it comes to helping your child learn the valuable lesson of responsibility. Providing your child with tasks on a regular basis is a great way of teaching self-reliance and encouraging pride in a job well done.

When your child has finished their task, make sure to acknowledge their efforts with, a hug, a thumbs-up, or a pat on the back. Always remember to tell them how much you appreciate the job they've done and how much they have helped you out.

Tip #3: Use Praise... and Be Specific!

Praising your children when they demonstrate positive character traits is a great way of reinforcing those characteristics you hope to develop.

For example, if helping your child to learn how to be a good friend and value strong friendships is important to you, making a practice of offering them specific praise is an excellent place to start.

It's natural to want to do more of the things for which we receive positive feedback. Make a point of telling your child what you think when they are comprehending or doing something kind or polite.

Another desirable trait that may be cultivated with the correct wording is honesty. When your child is honest about anything they've done or haven't done, praise them without reprimanding them by saying something like, "I like how you were honest about not finishing your schoolwork." Let's sit down and see what else needs to be done so you can get started right away.

Tip #4: Be the Best Role Model

Of course, modeling positive character characteristics in your own behavior is the best approach to help your child acquire positive character traits. After all, you are the most important role model for your child.

You must decide and vow to be the best example of those traits that you value most and want to instill in your child. If you make a habit out of practicing them, your child will surely notice — maybe not consciously at first, but rest assured that your actions will most definitely have a positive effect on a deeper level.

As you put this parenting advice into practice, remember that you're doing more than just raising a well-behaved child. You're raising a person who is responsible, kind and has a strong sense of right and wrong.

It is not always simple to assist your child in developing a strong moral character, but it is extremely gratifying. After all, your child will benefit from these values and talents for the rest of his or her life!

Technique 2: How to Understand Your Child Better

It's likely that after some time you will come to know what to expect from your child. But knowing what to expect from your teen is not enough — you have to take it one step further: you have to reach out and into their own world. This requires you to be able to understand them, understand their language, their points of view, and the problems they face on a daily basis, knowing what they want from you as a parent.

What are the Top Five Things the Teens Expect from Parents?

1. Being Loved and Accepted
2. Being Recognized and Validated
3. Freedom and Independence
4. Being Trusted

5.   Being Respected

Understanding your teen can be a daunting task at times. Your conversations may degenerate into name-calling, loud arguments, and miscommunication most of the time. Rather than feeling miserable, which only serves to perpetuate the pattern, focus on understanding what makes your child tick. Once you learn to communicate with them and acknowledge their feelings, it will be easier to understand them and go a step further to develop a long-lasting and productive relationship with them.

Tip #1: Maintain an Open Communication with Your Teen

You need to reconsider how you communicate with your teen. Is your communication centered on commands, complaints, and punishment? Do you have open communication in which you allow them to air their views and feelings freely? You will not be able to understand your child if you don't encourage them to talk.

You should be the one to start the conversation with an open-ended question. Ask your child or teen how their day in school was and continue asking more open-ended questions to encourage them to talk. If they're not in the mood, just let them know you are ready to listen to them when they feel ready.

Take advantage of the times you share together, like when you're in the car or setting the table for dinner, to open communication with them. Pay close attention to what they're saying and show genuine interest in their likes and passions. The main goal of this approach is simply to understand what motivates your child and makes them happy. It is about getting to understand their aspirations and inspirations.

Tip #2: Acknowledge Your Child's Feelings

It is important that your child knows that what they feel matters to you as a parent. They might get angry, frustrated, or embarrassed sometimes. Instead of brushing them off and telling them to stop overreacting, offer the support they need.

When you're having a heated argument, it's best to let your youngster speak. It's critical that you pay attention to them, nod, and maintain eye contact with them. If possible, you can even repeat what they said as a sign that you are actually listening and acknowledging their feelings. A hug is a magic and powerful thing that you may find very useful at times too.

Tip #3: Respect Your Child's Need for Independence

Every time your teen challenges your authority, it is important to understand that they are simply trying to demonstrate their independence. You have to keep in mind that your child is growing both physically and mentally. For them, this is the start of their independence.

This requires that you consider being flexible and give up a little control as mentioned before, it's a good idea to let them pick their own clothes, for example — both when shopping for new ones and when selecting what to wear for the day.

Independence also means respecting your child's privacy. If you didn't do so before, consider knocking before entering their room, asking for permission to come in, and giving them some time alone. If your child looks to be spending too much time alone, keep an eye on him or her. If your child seems withdrawn, take the time to talk to them and ask if they have a problem they would like to talk about.

Tip #4: Understand How the Brain of a Teen Works

As a parent, you must recognize that a teenager's brain is always changing. Once you recognize and appreciate this fact, you are more likely to understand and accommodate their behaviors. Because different parts of the brain mature at different rates, your teen's reactions might seem irrational to you.

In reality, the part associated with reward and motivation and impulsiveness matures much earlier than the part of the brain that is associated with the task of weighing the pros and the cons of every given action.

Consequently, your teen does not have the same view of the consequences of their actions as you do. With this in mind, it will be helpful that you discuss with your child the risk factors associated with risky decisions.

Technique 3: How to Educate and Guide Your Child to Make Good Decisions

A community's culture is its way of life. It refers to a group of people's socially transmitted habits, traditions, customs, and beliefs at any given moment.

More often than not, teenagers are likely to be left behind in catching up with the norms, values, behavior patterns, practices, etiquette, social groups, religion, superstitions, and spirituality among several other cultural concepts. There are several guides that can be helpful when orienting your teen into the cultural path you think might be best for them — always keeping in mind that they will ultimately make this choice for themselves.

Remain observant of your teen's behavior, their performance in school, and their relationships with their peers, friends, teachers, and other people in their inner circle. This, along with an open channel of communication, should help you to understand what problems your teen might be facing in regard to the world around them.

If their behavior seems different than normal in a way that is affecting them negatively, go back to the basics and try to re-establish communication with them. Find strategies to get your teen to talk to you about their concerns and open up to you. Getting a teen to open up is no easy feat, but employing the right techniques (being friendly, listening to them without judgment, offering support, etc.), is certainly an attainable goal.

It's time to offer some guidance after your child has opened up to you and told you about their problems. Express to them what choice you think is the best one for them, but always take the time to explain why you believe that choice to be the right one for them.

The Right Choices

Your teen needs to understand that their choices must always be in compliance with the provisions of local laws and regulations. Any illegal activities must be explained to them as such, as well as the consequences of taking part in them.

Situations you may have to deal with:

Situation #1: When Your Child Hasn't Come to a Decision

If your child or teen doesn't know what choice to make in any given situation, the one thing you absolutely must not do is try to impose your views on them. Instead, make time for both of you to analyze your child's problem and lay out what you consider to be the best solution or course of action to follow.

Consider comparing different solutions to a problem and try to explain the consequences or benefits that each of those solutions could carry. The most important thing is not to force your child to make a choice — let them mull over each potential solution, analyze the outcome, and ultimately make their own decision.

Situation #2: When Your Child Has Decided on a Course of Action

In some cases, your teen may already have made up their mind about how to solve a problem they're facing and all that's left is for them to carry out their decision. In that case, it's your role as a parent to show your love and support and offer to help them carry out their choice if they need it. This vote of confidence in your teen will make them feel trusted and will ensure that they come to you for their future problems.

Technique 4: How to Assist Your Child in Dismantling the Barriers That Separate Them from Their Families and Societies

Feeling "alone in a room full of people" is an exceedingly common emotion among teenagers. Your teen may start to feel like they don't fit in anywhere, which is a huge source of distress at this age. Teens need to feel like they belong and fit in with the world around them in order to get a sense of security and safety.

When your teen tells you "I don't fit in," what they're trying to say is "I don't feel safe." They feel different and alienated, which turns to anxiety. While this issue is likely more common in the school setting, teens can experience this feeling anywhere, even at home.

As a parent, you can do a lot to change the family environment — everything this book has talked about so far will help with that — but the truth is you can't make society adapt to your child. No matter how much you may want to change the world to fit them, the only thing you can do is work with your child and give them the social skills necessary to help them cope with this feeling of isolation.

Skill #1: Ensure That Your Child Feels Loved and Supported at Home

When teenagers feel rejected by their families, they tend to exhibit defiant behaviors. As such, as a parent of a teenager, you need to pay closer attention to your child and focus on understanding their feelings and desires.

Another good way to help your child feel included in the family is to organize activities that everyone participates in, like weekly family meetings, parties, or picnics. It is critical that each family member participates in an equitable manner. This way, your teen will be exposed to the importance of family unity

49

and it enables them to enjoy some much-needed solidarity, fun, attention, and love from family.

Skill #2: Teach Your Child to Be a Good Friend

There is no doubt that friendship is a crucial aspect of any child's development and growth. It is through playing and misunderstandings with friends that children learn skills like sharing, compromising problem-solving, forgiving, and most other social skills.

Teach your child empathy from an early age by being helpful in social events, making birthday cards for friends and family members, offering a helping hand to those younger than they and to the elderly. The skills they learn at home will naturally extend out into the world.

Skill #3: Tune into Your Child's Friendship Style

Some children thrive in large groups of friends, while others feel more comfortable with one or two kids at a time. It's crucial that you understand what works best for your child and not force them into social situations they find uncomfortable.

Keep in mind that what works for you may not necessarily work for them. If your child is happy playing with one friend, let them be, and don't force them to go to a big birthday party if it upsets them.

Skill #4: Open Your Home to Your Child's Friends

Make sure your child knows that your home is open to their friends. When they're younger, you can arrange playdates and have some activities prepared for them.

As your child begins to shift into adolescence, they will want to plan their own activities with their friends, but this doesn't mean they can't still go to your home. Let your teen know their friends are welcome any time and give them privacy and a safe space to have their fun.

Skill #5: Help Your Child Work through Family and Friendship Troubles

Misunderstandings are common among family members, friends, and peers. Your teen may need help from time to time in working through the emotions that arise from such conflicts. As private as teens tend to be, they may not immediately tell you about a fight or misunderstanding with a friend. Keep an eye out for any signs that your teen is distressed and try approaching them about it.

Depending on the severity of the conflict, your teen may even consider ending a friendship after a fight. In this case, it is not your role to step in and solve things for them. Rather, teach them the skills necessary to work through such situations. Draw on your own experience to show them that everyone fights sometimes, but that it is important to listen to the other person's side of the argument and try to be understanding. Explain the importance of not making a rash decision in the heat of the argument, and that it is preferable to wait until they've calmed down to try and solve the issue.

Skill #6 Encourage Your Child to Take Part in Extra-Curricular Activities

A great way to help a teen who is feeling isolated is to encourage them to engage in activities they enjoy. This could be anything from sports clubs to music or art programs — in school or out. This way, your child will be able to feel connected to other people their age who enjoy the same things.

Skill #7: Call in the Experts

If you believe that your teen's feelings of isolation and alienation are a matter of concern, don't hesitate to seek help from professionals. If not addressed early, severe feelings of isolation can result in depression and low self-esteem.

Technique 5: Put Yourself in Your Child's Shoes to Better Understand Them

During these trying years, your teen will be fighting many different battles at once. The best thing you can do as their parent is to offer support and understanding and show them that you're there for them. As much as possible, put yourself in their shoes. We were all teenagers once after all, and know full well what it's like to be in that position. Try to remember the things you wanted, thought, and felt when you were a teenager and keep that perspective close to your heart when helping your teen.

Remember that teenagers need help in learning how to manage their emotions. Don't lose your temper at your teen's emotional outbursts. Rather, try to keep your cool in order to make it easier to solve the conflict.

Your Teen Needs Space to Develop Their Personality

After a certain age, your teen will start to undergo a very rapid process of development. All the physical changes that are clearly visible are only the tip of the iceberg — it's the psychological changes that form the bulk of their developmental changes.

Provide Support

Be supportive by letting your teen develop their own personality and go through their own process of self-discovery. There are several occasions where your teen's emotions will overcome their better judgment. When that happens, allow them to vent their frustrations until they calm down. You do have to establish boundaries, however — if you don't tolerate name-calling, for example, this can be a good place to draw the line of what is allowed during their outbursts.

Being a teenager is not easy. This is a time when your child needs a lot of support from you. It is common to have a love-hate relationship with teens at times, but by offering your love and support, you will be on the right track to helping them get through these rough years.

Chapter 5. A Healthy Lifestyle for ODD Children and Teens

Mental and physical health are closely interlinked and one should never underestimate the power of a healthy lifestyle. However, can dietary requirements help children with behavioral issues like ODD or is this just a myth? Considering how many other disorders there are that are associated with ODD, and can be co-occurring, teaching your child to follow a healthy lifestyle is definitely not a bad idea. There are also specific nutrients that one can focus on to improve the brain's ability to function and your child's overall mood that is worth mentioning. And, why not incorporate some healthy movement into their hobbies and activities? This chapter takes a look at how to best approach nutrition and physical health for your ODD child and teen, and it will also provide some great family-time ideas with a happy ending in mind.

Dietary Requirements — Are There Any?

Although a medical practitioner will most likely refer you to a therapist or in a more serious scenario prescribe medication, claims of taking specific nutrients in the form of supplements have surfaced in discussions and articles. In these articles, writers claim that the use of specific nutrients is effective and worth trying if your child is struggling with severe ODD symptoms. Nutrients are present in food, and they are also available in supplement form. The discussion below will focus on when you should consider a supplement and how you can look for nutrient-rich foods that provide the good stuff in the most natural way possible.

Omega 3 Fatty Acids

Omega 3 is an all-around miracle worker, and ADHD patients are known to take a concentrated form of Omega 3 to help with their symptoms. This is because this fatty acid, which the body cannot create itself, is a crucial nutrient for the maintenance and, in the case of children, the development of the brain. Omega 3 fatty acids don't only help for ADHD, it has a myriad of pros when it comes to ailments concerning brain function that affects young and old alike. It is also considered to be a crucial nutrient required by humans, but it is not available in a wide range of foods. This is why many people choose to take an Omega 3 supplement to make up for its deficit in our modern diet. Omega 3 contains two types of fatty acids called DHA and EPA. Both are vital for optimal brain function and development from childhood, but EPA is especially therapeutic when it comes to mental health issues. To use Omega 3 for therapeutic measures such as treating symptoms of ADHD or ODD, look for specific fish oil or supplement that has a higher EPA than DHA ratio. The recommended ratio is at least twice the amount of EPA as DHA.

One of the issues Omega 3 fatty acids have been studied to relieve and improve is anxiety. A study conducted at the China Medical University Hospital, where subjects were compared by either being administered Omega 3 polyunsaturated fats or placebos, provided a surprising result as patients who were administered Omega 3 indicated significant decreases in their anxiety levels. Anxiety is a component that is prevalent not only in ODD but in most of its co-occurring conditions. Apart from this, considering that your child's brain will be growing throughout childhood and adolescence and that Omega 3 fatty acids are crucial for neural development apart from having these benefits for children and teens that have ODD, it seems almost strange that there is not a community van driving around in the streets bellowing, "Remember to give your children their daily dose of Omega 3 fatty acids" through a crackling megaphone (Demko, 2018).

What Would We Do Without Good Ol' Omega 3?

Don't Forget about Vitamin E!

This is true. We can't forget about Vitamin E because it helps absorb Omega 3! That's the most important reason. However, since we're here, let's take a look and see if Vitamin E has any other benefits of note.

Vitamin E appears to have many benefits and important functions that include improved vision, healthy blood, healthy skin, and a healthy brain. Vitamin E is also a rich source of antioxidants, which protect human cells against the damage of free radicals. The good news about Vitamin E is that it's not as scarce in our everyday diet as Omega 3 fatty acids are. You can get your Vitamin E by consuming peanuts, olive oil, canola oil, almonds, or even meat and dairy products. So, even though Vitamin E helps you get the best from your super powered Omega 3, it also has its own benefits. And, for a child, it is not necessary to provide a supplement if you give them a good old peanut butter sandwich on a regular basis (Mayo Clinic Staff, 2020).

Zinc

Zinc has a really interesting benefit. While studies were conducted on children with ADHD, researchers found that they had lower levels of zinc than children who don't have ADHD, and hypothesized that there may be a possible link. Today, we know that zinc can have a therapeutic effect for children and teens who have ODD as it can decrease levels of impulsivity, hyperactivity, but strangely enough, not any aspect related to inattentiveness. It is also important to note that zinc is known as an essential nutrient just like Omega 3 fatty acids, which means that the human body doesn't produce this nutrient. If your child or teen with ODD displays any of these two symptoms, which are not only common in ODD but also in co-occurring conditions, you can visit your doctor and ask that a check is done on your child's zinc levels. This may solve a problem that you previously didn't know how to solve and that didn't show results under therapy alone. Zinc levels that are too low can be problematic, but so can levels that are too high. So, if you are considering giving your child an extra supplement, the best decision is to first consult your doctor.

Magnesium

Magnesium is one of the most abundant minerals in the body, and most people are not aware of the multiple functions it has in ensuring physical and mental health. That being said, Magnesium is also not as prevalent in our modern diet of processed and flavored foods as it used to be, so many people have a magnesium deficiency without them knowing it. A study in 2017 reviewed 18 previous studies conducted on magnesium and the researchers concluded that magnesium does, in fact, have a therapeutic effect on anxiety. This is because magnesium works with our muscles, our brain, and our nervous system and it regulates a part of the brain called the hypothalamus. The hypothalamus regulates two glands in your brain called the pituitary and the adrenal glands, and these glands are responsible for regulating your anxiety levels. Apart from anxiety, there are other great reasons for one to focus on maintaining healthy magnesium levels. For example, it helps with muscular pain and relaxation, it can give you a great night's sleep, improves your mood, keeps your blood pressure normal, and can be used to treat migraines.

If you want to first try to improve your child's magnesium intake through their diet, then there are foods you can incorporate that are high in magnesium. These foods include leafy greens like kale and spinach, avocado, legumes, dark chocolate, nuts and seeds, and sticking to whole grains. If you want to look for ways to reduce stress and anxiety naturally, you can try pushing up the magnesium intake in your child's diet or consult a doctor about a supplement. Magnesium truly is a super mineral (Ferguson, 2019; Additude, 2016).

Apart from focusing on these helpful nutrients, it is important to understand the dangers of the high-sugar, processed food diet if your child has a mental or behavioral disorder. Sugar wreaks havoc in a child's system who struggles with their mood, behavior, hyperactivity, and when eating only refined carbohydrates, one can hardly expect to get any of that zinc from the snowy white hamburger bun you just gave them to eradicate. Following 80% whole foods and a 20% what-kids-love-to-eat food, approach can help to balance out nutritional issues you were not aware of, which can lead to behavioral improvement.

The 80/20 Principle

Children don't want to be on a constant health journey, so the 80/20 principle is a great way to treat them every now and then if you are focused on giving them a nutritious eating plan. The 80/20 principle means that you eat well 80% of the time and you treat yourself 20% of the time. It's just the right ratio to stay healthy and satisfied. If you were to put this into practice, it would mean that the kids can have a small-to-medium-sized candy bar one or two times a week, and on Friday night the family can have pizza and ice cream. The rest of the week will be spent eating nutrient-rich foods. If you think my 20% is a little sparse, which it maybe is, you can up the treats a tiny bit. It's important for your children to enjoy healthy food as well as their treats, and if your kids are still young, you've got the ball in your hands. Little ones are easy to teach good eating habits because habits are difficult to change when a child gets older. So, if your child is used to more junk food, they are going to give you a very hard time if you try to implement the 80/20. But, don't let that faze you. Nutritious foods can also taste good; once you get them off the preservatives and salt and they get their taste buds back, they'll be more compliant. Have some fun with the 80/20 by asking your kids what they want as treats each week. Just make sure they understand the relative size the treat's supposed to be, and you'll end up with a satisfied bunch. If you are looking for some information about clean eating and whole foods, you can read about the clean eating philosophy and how you can magically turn some junk food favorites into whole food options by reading right below.

The Whole Foods and Clean Eating Philosophy

What do all of these phrases mean? Is clean eating what you do and whole foods what you do it too? Or are they basically the same concept? I think I may be confusing everyone, including myself, so let's start again:

"Whole foods" is a term that is usually applied to foods like fruits, vegetables, whole grains, and legumes that have undergone minimal to no processing. However, animal products can also be classified as "whole foods." The problem comes in when you want to classify foods that are not completely processed but they are also not completely 'whole' anymore. It appears that there are several phases or layers of processing that make very few foods 100% whole food — only those you pluck directly from a tree, in fact. This is because even processes like washing and chopping are seen as processing just like canning and preserving foods would be seen as processing. But there's a big difference between just washing food and canning it; with canned foods, you add preservatives and additives to make it last longer. So, this is where the crux of the distinction lies; not all food processing procedures are equal.

In fact, the phrases "minimally-processed" and "ultra-processed" were invented to help us just in case we become confused. Minimally-processed food refers to food that has undergone processing that left the food close to its natural state. In this case, washing would be a good example; the dirt and pesticides were washed from the food, but there was nothing added to change the composition of the food in itself. This also means that the food maintains most of its original nutritional value if it is only minimally processed. As minimal-processing moves to ultra-processing, ingredients like salt, sugar, and fat are added, which causes a decrease in the food's nutritional value.

This basically means that it's not possible to eat a 100% clean diet, but that eating foods that are minimally processed and that still resembles their most natural state is the best way to provide the most nutrients you can from food to your family and to children who need to focus on nutrients and nourishment. Here are some examples of how you can make simple whole food swaps from previously processed options:

- Instead of using white bread, swap it for bread that is whole grain or a whole meal.

- Chuck away the Cheerios and give your child a bowl of steel-cut oats with fresh banana or blueberries.

- Trade in the snack bar for a handful of unsalted, mixed nuts.

- Try to stick to fresh, free-range chicken instead of purchasing protein from the deli section.

- When you visit the grocery store again, opt for fresh fruit instead of buying fruit juice; it contains so much more fiber and provides the correct amount of fructose per serving.

There are other options you can consider too, like swapping your white basmati rice for the brown version, trying to rather make something from scratch than buying the pre-made version. There's not always enough time for this, but every small step makes a difference. And, teaching your child to love whole foods from a young age will likely cause the habit to stick as they grow older, making them strong and healthy adults. Consider the 80/20 principle, and have some fun in the kitchen. (Health Agenda, 2017).

Productive Activities and Hobbies

When we talk about productive activities and hobbies for children and teens with ODD, what we are actually referring to is activities that will provide extra aid in subduing the aggression and defiance and that will promote a sense of physical and mental relief, decreased anxiety, and an improved mood. Exercise is one of the most widely researched natural aids for depression and anxiety because it is a virtually free alternative to expensive therapy sessions and, in some cases, medication. What research has found regarding exercise, however, is that normal low-intensity movement may keep a healthy person mentally in shape, but when an individual suffers from a condition or a disorder like depression or anxiety, a higher intensity level of exercise is required to get that same benefit. This is most likely due to the brain of a person who has depression or anxiety's inability to produce enough of the required neurotransmitters when doing the same amount of exercise, as a healthy person would.

The Benefits of Organized Sport

When it comes to the requirements you are looking for exercise, your child or teen's activities and hobbies, one of the best options out there is participating in organized sport. It's almost like a tailor-made treatment program for a child with conduct and behavioral issues. Let's look at the benefits sports offer children in general without considering they may have a disorder like ODD:

Apart from sport being an excellent way to stay active and to exercise on high-intensity and low-intensity levels, there are so many other benefits parents should know about. There are team sports and individual sports, and each one has its own unique qualities. The trick is to pick the type of sport that is right for your child, which can ultimately help change their attitude, their outlook on life, the way they react towards rules and boundaries, and their overall development as human beings. Let's look at the general benefits of playing sports that are applicable to all children and teens first.

Children, especially those who play sports from a young age and continue to play throughout their childhood, are prone to have a well-developed vision, and they are also less likely to develop vision problems. Then, of course, playing sports is one way to keep your child healthy and help them to maintain a healthy weight for their age. Studies indicate that children who are active, specifically those who participate in an activity after school, are more likely to maintain a normal weight. Then, your child will be able to develop and fine-tune their coordination and motor skills just by learning to play and participating in organized sports. Motor skills and coordination come in handy doesn't matter where you are in your life — even when you're driving a car, and children who have participated in organized sports generally have a very well-developed sense of coordination and good motor skills.

Then, if you find your youngster a sport that fits their dynamics and personality, the sense of team spirit and positive relationships they will develop with teammates and coaches can develop self-identify and boost their self-esteem. It's almost like recreating the family teamwork dynamics at home, and it also has a very rewarding goal for kids when they work together and reach their team's goals. What a priceless quality to learn that can support a child to reach a healthy state of mind as an adult that can ultimately get them far in their life journey.

What's left? Well, fun and friendship! This one may be tricky for your ODD youngster or teen as they are also likely to show disrespect towards their peers. However, if they are able to find friendship in this venture, it will be life-changing for them.

After looking at these pros, which are applicable outcomes for all children who participate in organized sports, how do you choose a sport that's right for your child? Firstly, they need to be into the idea of playing a sport. My young one had an affinity for karate because she thought it was all about fighting. To her surprise, it was not about fighting at all; it was about restraint and respect. Nevertheless, she was willing to make the mental shift as she enjoyed the educational and physical aspects of the sport, so I knew that we had found the right activity for her. After picking her up from a lesson, she would be calmer, more open to suggestions and instruction, and she would sleep better.

However, that's not what we're here for. We are here to focus on your child and their health, so let's look at our options.

The first aspect to look at when you are looking at different sports options is what your child or teen is generally interested in. Even better, if your child has an interest in a specific sport, this can make the process easier. On the other hand, being interested in or enjoying watching a specific sport doesn't mean you'd want to play that sport, just like some girls like to watch football. So, let's dig a bit deeper.

What do you think is your child's biggest mental or emotional need at this point that can be satisfied through playing a sport? For example, if your child is not a team-sports kind of person, there may not be any sense in looking into these options, and you may find better results looking at options like tennis, squash, track, or another type of sport where your child competes as an individual. Some children enjoy individual sports because the focus shifts from teamwork to developing an inner sense of individual drive that can be great for learning about perseverance and self-belief.

It is also important to only take into account sports that will match the abilities of your child. For example, some children have co-occurring disorders like ADHD or they can even have conditions like asthma that may affect which sports they are compatible with. It's important to inform the coach about your child or teen's conditions, whether they are mental or physical. When you and your child have found a sport, they want to try out, put the foundation or sports organization that is responsible for organizing and training through your own assessment process. Ask yourself the following questions regarding the sports club or organization you and your child are looking to join:

Does this program have a vision and a mission that matches your own or are there clashes in your beliefs or views, and the ones of the program or organization?

What level of involvement does the organization expect from you as a parent?

Do the practice and game schedules match your and your child's schedules?

How do the coaches select team members? Do you agree with the selection process, and do you think it is fair?

Is there adequate supervision and do the coaches and management team appear to be responsible and experienced?

Is the program well-organized or do they just go with the flow?

Finally, does the program or organization have some sort of insurance that can cover any injuries sustained by your child whilst training or during a game?

If any of these points are of interest or importance to you, I suggest you create a list of selection criteria and use it to choose the best organization or club your child can join. If you live in a smaller area and the setting is more informal but you know most of the people involved, then most of these criteria may not be necessary. You can choose which ones you want to use (Stanford Children's Health, 2019).

Sports have shown to be specifically effective and therapeutic for children and teens who have ADHD. Because ADHD and ODD are so closely related, studying the benefits can also bring some final insight into the physical and mental benefits that have been recorded through research and ongoing studies.

Athletic skills have been called an "island of competence" your child can use to develop a level of resilience and high self-esteem that can help them deal with their diagnosis. For children who have ADHD, individual sports that are focused on developing and mastering a specific skill are especially beneficial. Examples include martial arts, swimming, archery, ballet, and even diving. This element of focus is great for improving their sense of concentration and focus and the physical aspect helps them to get rid of excess energy. One of the best things about sport for a child that has to deal with the diagnosis of a disorder is the sense of achievement and accomplishment they get from it. There is no equivalent to how valuable this is for the development of their self-worth and self-esteem, which can, in many cases, be the reason they lash out (CHADD, 2018).

Artistic Endeavors

Expressive activities like art can also be very therapeutic for children with ODD. Just like you're expressing yourself physically when playing sports, some children or teens may be more suited to expressing themselves emotionally or artistically. You can talk to your child about attending an extra-curricular art class or you can take them to an art shop and buy some supplies so they can experiment at home. If possible, create their own little art space where they can practice their creativity. Good options are acrylic paints as they are water-based and quick-drying as opposed to oil paint, which takes forever to dry and is very hard to clean once it messes. You can also buy them a set of drawing pencils, charcoal, a sketch pad, and a canvas or two. They can purchase an eBook that contains tutorials or watch YouTube tutorials on how to create landscapes, seascapes, impressionist paintings, realist images — you name it.

When they've created something that you know they've worked hard on and you know they are proud of, frame it and put it up against the wall where everyone can see it. This act of appreciation will do wonders for their self-esteem.

Writing a Tell-all

I think all children who struggle emotionally and psychiatrically should have a diary. In fact, everyone struggles, so everyone can benefit from having a diary. Some people just enjoy writing more than others, just like some people enjoy painting more than others. Writing is another therapeutic way of getting pent-up energy out of your system — energy that may have been unfairly projected on a family member. Just as you would have bought your child proper art supplies, buy them a nice diary. Buy them one with a cover that they will like; one that they will enjoy opening and writing in every day. And add a special pen. You can even make a pact with them that, every time they feel like acting out, they first have to write down how they are feeling in their diary before acting out. Tell them that the diary belongs to them and that no one will read it so they can write whatever they want in it, as long as they write how they feel at that moment.

That diary may look a bit worn down after a few months, but that doesn't matter. When it's full, tell your child to store it in a special place and get them a brand new one.

Positive Reinforcement

While we're on the topic of raising healthy ODD munchkins or larger versions of them, let's look at ways they can be encouraged to develop healthy habits. One way to sneakily work on changing your child or teen's habits is by using behavior modification techniques. I know, it kind of sounds like you'd have to strap your child to a chair and put electrodes all over their forehead and temples and push a big red button. However, the simplicity of the reality may shock you. If you want to modify the behavior of your ODD child or teen, a very effective way to do so is by using positive reinforcement. From an ODD child's perspective, they are usually expecting a scolding, a reprimanding, or a punishment as a response to their destructive behavior. So, if this method doesn't involve strapping them to a chair or any type of furniture for that matter and it is still effective, how does it work? Positive reinforcement has shown to improve misbehaviors like acting aggressively towards others and violating or breaking rules. It also encourages social-friendly behaviors like following directions and (willingly) sharing with others.

Another reason for applying positive reinforcement is to help your child develop a sense of responsibility by doing their chores, completing their homework, and getting along with other family members without arguing or being difficult about it. Let's take this step-by-step and start by looking at the theory behind genius.

Would you get up and go to work every day and most likely work late once or twice a week if you didn't get a paycheck at the end of the month? I'm not referring to work for charity organizations here — I'm talking about your average primal 9–5 daily grind most people go through to keep food on the table, minus the occasional feel-good moment when you show your colleague how to plug in their computer. Well, let me tell you, I most certainly won't. What's the point of going through all that sweat, tears, and stress if there's no reward or payoff? What's that 'thing' called that keeps us going to work every day? That's basically positive reinforcement. In adult terms, it's another word for remuneration, but how does it translate into ODD child/teen language?

Firstly, like adults, kids are wired the same way; if they receive positive reinforcement for their good behavior, they will maintain this behavior. The same goes for hard work; positive reinforcement will motivate a child to maintain a certain standard in their work if they know that they will be rewarded for it. Here are examples of how you can implement positive reinforcement in very simple ways for smaller children to more sneaky and complicated ways for older children and teens who would want expensive stuff:

- Cheering and clapping will work on the youngsters. A teenager may think it's the lamest and most embarrassing thing that's ever happened to them, which I, personally, would find quite amusing.

- A good high-five can go both ways, depending on the context. Try not to high-five your teen in front of their friends, though. They may, however, value it as a private celebration moment between the two of you.

- Hugging is a great way to reinforce your child because of its affectionate nature. This approach will work very well with youngsters and it will help satisfy their appetite for affection and attention. Sometimes an ODD child will resist this type of affection, but in the context of achievement and approval, it will most likely be a great success.

- Now, here is something you can also apply to your teens. It involves spending some special time together. So, of course, your little one would like to go out for ice cream, but you can also take your teen out for lunch or dinner or coffee. Take the time to say uplifting things to your child and have a laugh. And a slice of cherry pie.

- Why don't you try talking positively about your child, in front of your child, with another adult? For example, "Jenny painted the most beautiful picture of a still life yesterday. Yes, she even arranged and designed the still life herself! I'm getting it framed for the living room." Your child will feel like the most important person in the world!

- In other situations, you can give them tangible rewards or extra privileges — these work well with older children. For example, you can extend your teen's curfew by an hour as a reward for good behavior or compliance with the house rules. Or, you can give your little one some extra TV time or video game time.

Praise

Praise is also a fantastic way to apply positive reinforcement, and there are different ways you can use praise to increase its effectiveness. Kids often act out because, when they actually exhibit any form of good behavior, it sometimes goes unnoticed, which makes them feel that they are doing it in vain. We can't exactly expect a child to do their chores for the sake of the greater good, now can we? The ironic part of all of this is that negative behavior is what gets the most attention from parents, where it should actually be the opposite. If two children were gallivanting around the house but one is jumping on and ruining your new leather couch while the other is just sweetly building a Lego castle, which one will most likely get your attention? I think we'll all start by frantically trying to get the wild one off the couch. The other one, however, also needs to be recognized for their good manners. What if you turned the situation around and focused on praising the good behavior and ignoring the couch-hopping? There would be two children quietly sitting and playing with Lego in no time. If you give your child positive feedback on what they are doing, they are likely to act out, and by applying this technique to an ODD child or teen, you may be able to influence their pattern of outbursts to become less frequent and even diminish the triggers that cause them.

Behaviors that are especially responsive to praise are very similar to those that react well to positive reinforcement; this is probably because verbal praise is a form of positive reinforcement. Let's go through behaviors that are specifically responsive to praise:

Firstly, there is prosocial behavior again. If your child or teen is willing to take turns without fighting, use positive or kind words, is willing to share with others, and makes an effort to get along with others in general, these are all actions that respond well to praise, and praising your child in these situations can create a pattern of reinforced behavior. Then, if your child shows any form of compliance, which is usually a rare scenario if you have an ODD child or teen, this behavior reacts successfully to praise. Compliance can include following general rules, following instructions set by an authoritative figure, and even just minding their own business when they could've been participating in naughty and destructive behavior. Finally, an action that should be in the least acknowledged and praised is when your ODD child shows that they are making an effort; even better if they are making an effort to improve in areas that need improvement. Even if they are not quite there yet, praising their efforts will motivate them to keep trying and to stay strong.

Now that we've looked at situations that partner well with praise, it is also important to focus on strategically applying praise to get the maximum effect and reinforcement from it. Funnily enough, if praise is not given appropriately, it can be unhealthy for your child's perception of themselves and their abilities, which can be damaging for them when they enter the world as adults. By looking at the following examples of healthy methods, the unhealthy ones will most likely become clear to you as well.

Firstly, provide realistic praise. We all think that our children are the smartest, most beautiful, and most special children on the planet, but telling them this too often may not be too good for them. For example, instead of saying, "Maggie, you are the best ballet dancer I've ever seen," try to identify an actual positive feat that you can encourage and focus on that. For example, change it to "you really did a great job with your pirouettes; I can see that you've been practicing hard!" If the praise is actually applicable to an aspect or technique that your child has been working on, they will feel even more validated and loved because they know that you've been paying attention and that you noticed the improvement.

Linking closely to the above approach, constructive praise includes avoiding labeling your child. Labeling is just a short version of providing exaggerated or non-specific praise. Even if this is your honest opinion and your child may have an IQ of 140+, it's not productive to call him "Mommy's little genius." An old school friend of mine decided to become a medical doctor, and, when her mother refers to her or talks about her, she doesn't call her by her name — she actually talks about "my daughter that's a doctor." Every single time. Which do you think your child would prefer, for their parents to acknowledge them as a person or to identify them by their highly-acclaimed profession? This is an example of how this type of praise can go horribly wrong and actually be bad for your child even though your intentions are to show love and appreciation.

Then, you can get the most out of praising your child by being specific when you praise them. Most of us say "great job" and assume that our children understand what we are referring to. However, enunciation has an effect on how a child interprets praise. You can say "well done" or you can say "well done for remembering to take out the trash!" Personally, I'd appreciate the second one because I know what I'm being praised for.

Now, here's an interesting one that I've come across when socializing with other parents who have children. It's almost as if the concept of praise is not understood completely. A parent would praise their child, but they would include a negative phrase or connotation within the message. It reminds me of how my grandmother approached the concept of praise; I once told her that I got a good score on a test, and she responded by saying, "Well, now you can make it even better next time." Is there actually praise in there somewhere? I never told her anything about my test scores again. From my perspective as a child, a good score was not really acknowledged in the praise, but I realized later in my life that it was implied.

However, implied praise is not enough for a child. It is the same with giving praise, which is supposed to be a positive experience and message but lacing it with negativity or scorn. For example, "I'm proud of you for not trying to ruin dinner." The duality in that sentence will not motivate your child and their focus will immediately fall on the latter part of the sentence, which contains negative wording. Your child's thoughts will most likely be, "Oh, Mom or Dad thinks I always ruin dinner. Great." This can possibly backfire and cause negative reinforcement. Instead, you can try "I'm proud of you for being so positive and chatting with everyone at the dinner table tonight." What's your opinion on this? Have you ever caught yourself giving praise to your child that is laced with negativity? When dealing with an ODD child or teen, your child's repeated misbehavior and aggression can program your brain into a negative copilot mode, and negative words will subsequently leave your mouth spontaneously, even if you want to communicate a positive message. This is completely understandable. So, this specific part of how praise can be effective if used strategically is one that parents with troubled children, like children and teens with ODD, should pay attention to.

Finally, with the focus on children with behavioral disorders, you can superpower your praise and boost their self-esteem by praising their effort and not its outcome. The outcome will not always be successful, but you can always praise your child for making an effort. They will be motivated to step up that effort, and this can eventually lead them to success. How proud can a parent be of a child that keeps on trying, even if they are struggling? They deserve acknowledgment and praise from those who love them most (Morin, 2019).

Organizing Constructive Family Time

When it comes to organizing some family time, there are lots of things you and your family can do, depending on what everyone enjoys doing and focusing on activities that will improve family dynamics and relationships. Here are some goals to consider when looking at different family activities:

Firstly, the activity will be ideal if it fits into your family's team goal or vision. For example, if one of your goals is to improve relationships between the siblings, then setting an activity that promotes this goal is ideal.

Secondly, organizing an activity that everyone will enjoy will also help a lot. Your ODD child and especially your ODD teen may act like there's nothing that interests them, but don't let it faze you. By observing your child's everyday activities, you will definitely have a clear idea of their interests, likes, and dislikes.

Finally, maintain a balance between the type of activities that you'd like your family to partake in. For example, try not to plan all of them to be at home or in front of the TV. Try going outdoors or doing something active, and change the scenery a bit. You know your family — have some fun! Consider these examples as a basis that which you can build your own authentic activities:

A Movie Night with a Twist

How diverse is your family in terms of age? Do you have teens and tweens? Are there some conflicting ideas when it comes to everyone's favorite movie? I know what it's like watching a movie someone else is absolutely crazy about and you just want to fall asleep. However, movie nights can be fun bonding experiences. Well, if you have tiny tweens, move choices are going to be more limited, but otherwise, each family member gets to search Netflix, choose a movie, and throw all the movie names in a hat. Or a plastic container if you don't have a sturdy hat. Make sure that nobody can see the names by writing them on paper and folding the paper in half, leaving the blank sides showing. Then, schedule a day every week or every second week when the family will come together for movie night — no excuses!

Each night, make one person's favorite snacks (you can create a separate hat containing everyone's preferences and draw one each time if you want) put the mattresses down on the floor in front of the TV to make sure there's space for everyone, and get comfy. You can even decide to wear your pajamas every time you have a movie night. Focus on a constructive conversation and make sure that everyone's opinions and comments are treated equally.

Keeping Active

There really is no better way to remind your children about how precious nature is than stuffing them all in the car and taking them on a family hike. If you live near scenic nature reserves or hiking spots, this is a great activity for your family that will also allow everyone to get some exercise. You can incorporate activities like bird-watching, photography, and getting to know the different trees and plants that grow in your area. If there's a lake in the area, go swimming or tanning — your kids will love that. You can play games on the beach and have a picnic.

On the other hand, if you're only going for a hike, you can also have a picnic or you can take everyone out to lunch when it gets too hot to be outside. If it's winter, you can take everyone ice skating — there really is a lot to do outdoors. If you want to go on one of those extreme family team-building ventures where everyone slides off a cliff, please be careful. And, stay hydrated!

Let's Do Some Good

This option is highly recommended. It will teach the whole family a lot about giving back to society, about appreciating each other and what you have, and it will inspire you to work even harder to become a tightly-knit group of individuals who love and respect one another. Volunteer work is not something that is done by a lot of people, and organizations like homeless shelters and animal shelters always need volunteers. Even old-age homes will always appreciate an extra hand — not to mention all the elderly that live there who haven't seen their relatives for so long.

Making a difference in the lives of others can teach you a lot about yourself, especially your ODD child or teen. For example, they may realize that they have a lot of struggles in their life, but they also have a lot to be thankful for, like a family who supports them, a roof over their heads, and a yummy meal ready when they're home from school. It's truly heartwarming to show compassion to someone else. If your children like animals, take them to a shelter and let them play with and feed the animals. Some animals become really stressed if they are in a small enclosure for too long, so if you have older children or teens, you can organize for them to take the animals for walks or play with them outside their enclosures. For a child who hates authority and automatically rebels against it, how will it feel to work with those who have so much less than they do? It can have a huge impact on their frame of reference, and the whole experience can make you stronger as a family.

The Dinner Co-op

I could do with some pizza right now. Not the type that's delivered at your doorstep in 15 minutes — that pizza you make in your own kitchen where you start with the dough, chop up all the toppings, and watch it slowly cook in the oven with your mouth watering. Does your family like pizza? Have you ever made your own pizza at home? It's the best because you can put anything you like on your pizza. Involving the whole family in making dinner and creating it into a family tradition is a productive way of strengthening family bonds and, there are activities that require all skill levels from washing the vegetables to frying the bacon and kneeing the dough.

You don't have to make pizza, though. That was just the first thought that popped into my head, probably because I'm a bit peckish. If you have a specific cultural dish you enjoy as a family, then what a wonderful way to bring everyone together to work as a team. And the best part is enjoying the feast that all of you worked on afterward.

Beautiful Parent, Take Note

These activities are meant to be fun, empowering, and emotionally valuable to your family. However, you are constantly aware that you have a child or teen present that can blow up, defy instruction, and act negatively. For this reason, it is crucial to always be in control of the situation. If it's you and your partner, you can work as a team to keep the atmosphere the way you want it to. It's important to use positive reinforcement equally on all your children and not let it stand out that the whole operation is "Operation ODD." Your children may sense that and their reaction to your positive attempts may flip them around and worsen the situation. This is one of the most important things to keep in mind if you have an ODD child or teen. In the beginning, before you start implementing some of the behavioral techniques we discussed, you will still be walking on that thin line, not knowing when, why, or how the explosion will occur. What makes you a powerful parent is that you can rise above this, understand that it's something that can happen, but you can work toward making a massive improvement in your child's life.

To receive your FREE eBook "ADHD Organizing Solutions"

Scan this QR Code

Chapter 6. How to Discipline my ODD Child or Teenager

We've all been through this. We've tried multiple strategies with the aim to discipline our ODD child or teen without becoming emotional, angry, overly upset, or just plain losing it. If you've done a lot of research and tried many approaches, chances are that you may have tried one that would've eventually worked, but the hard part is to stick to it when your child or teen is being so incredibly difficult. And the most infuriating and unfathomable part of dealing with an ODD child or teen is that, even though you, as the parent, need to remind yourself that it is a condition and that your child's destructive and abrasive behaviors are not who they really are, they still seem to know exactly how and when to push your buttons and will never hesitate to do so when they lash out.

This is what leaves ODD parents so tired, defeated, and sometimes even completely depressed; wrapping your head around that paradox is not easy, and parents that deal with this on a daily basis should be commended for actively trying to understand their child's situation while being under constant attack. There are two key components to effectively disciplining an ODD child or teen. The first is using techniques that have proven to be effective and that are not emotionally harmful to your child. Secondly, and this is where most parents falter just because it is so incredibly hard: consistency. Don't leave even a crack open where your child can identify a gap and take their chances to act out. Start by considering these fundamental strategies you can implement in your household to tame your child's aggression and anger by drastically limiting their opportunities to misbehave.

Fundamental Strategies

Let's state the facts. Children and teenagers with ODD are blatantly and unabashedly disrespectful, confrontational, and disobedient. So, how do you curb this destructive behavior that is affecting everyone in your household? Understanding their behavior and reacting based on that understanding is key.

Positive Attention

First, one of the things that can make ODD behavior worse is if the child sees that they are negatively reprimanded more than their siblings. This essentially means that their brain will wire itself to think their siblings always get positive attention and they always get negative attention, which can cause feelings of bitterness or jealousy, and these feelings are going to worsen their behavior. So, when you see your child or teen acting up, try to stop what you are doing to give them your attention for at least fifteen minutes. Try to smother the aggression and defiance with positivity and affection, and depending on their age, do a quick activity with them or ask them to do something that will make them feel special. This approach is almost the same as one we've previously discussed where the negative behavior of the child is completely ignored. However, in this case, you will use this approach if you know that the behavior exhibited may be due to neurological interplay, for example, ADHD acting up or if you could see that your child was clearly triggered.

The Behavior Plan/Reward System

The second strategy can be successfully linked to the first one to create a multifaceted prevention approach. The second strategy is to create an action and consequence behavior plan that you can discuss with your child. This will work well if your child is old enough to understand the concept, but considering the general age range of children diagnosed with ODD, it is unlikely that your child will be too young.

Start creating the plan by identifying the behavioral issues that need to be addressed. These issues can range from acting aggressively towards you, your partner, or siblings, refusing to follow any orders or doing schoolwork, shouting or saying nasty things, throwing tantrums, or misbehaving at school. After you've identified the pressing behaviors, you need to identify fitting consequences that are aimed at improving your child's understanding of their behavior but also not breaking down their self-esteem. There could be rewards if they behave and maybe some extra chores if they don't. A reward system is something that has been tried out in a disciplinary strategy for ODD children, and it has proven to be successful over and over again. There are different types of reward systems parents use, and many parents come up with their own unique ideas and systems that fit their household requirements. However, there are also systems that already have established procedures and rules, like the token economy system that works well with ODD children and teens, so let's take a look at this reward system as an example.

How to Create a Token Economy System in Your Household

A token economy system is known as one of the most effective ways to get any child to follow your house rules, and this includes children with ODD.

However, there may still be a slight delay in compliance if your child has ODD, but the success has been proven. This system works like an action-and-consequence behavior plan, but it has a built-in rewards system. Your children earn tokens for reaching specific goals on a daily, bi-daily, or weekly basis, and the tokens work almost like a monetary system that they can use to claim or buy bigger rewards. If your child is still in kindergarten, you can consider using a sticker chart as they really enjoy this format, but if your child is older, the tokens work very well. Let's say, for example, you want your child to complete their homework in the afternoon, come home from school with no complaints from their teachers, go a week without any temper tantrums, or do their chores. They can earn tokens for doing what is expected of them, and these tokens then have a specific value. Linked to earning the tokens, you can have a system indicating what they can "earn" or which rewards they can get with x number of tokens. These rewards can start small for a small number of tokens and can become more valuable and covetable for a larger number of tokens. By choosing rewards that you know your children love, they'll be motivated to behave, get the tokens, and save up for their rewards. So, if we want to create a token economy, where do we start?

- Keep it simple. Parents can get really hyped up about creating a rewards system or a token economy system, and this can result in lots of planning and an elaborate setup, which ends up looking almost like a business pitch! The problem is, it is going to completely confuse your child. Approach the creation of the system by looking at it from your child's perspective; you know your child better than anyone, so as long as you keep in mind that the system is being created for your child and why it's being created, your efforts will most likely be wildly successful.

- Now, you need to determine the goals your child needs to achieve in order to earn tokens. Pour yourself a glass of wine and mull over this for a while. You don't want your child to think that some good behavior is more valuable or 'better' than others; you'd rather want to create the impression that all good behavior is equal. If you want to give your child tokens of different values for different goals without creating this impression, you can place the focal point on effort. Alternatively, all tokens can have the same value, and your child will just have to save longer for larger rewards; it doesn't have to be that complicated.

- Next, a component that is important to consider is to not only focus on bad behavior and give your ODD child goals that are tough to achieve. They are going to struggle with most of their behavioral goals, and they will need motivation by earning tokens for other behavior or activities that they do not find as difficult to complete or achieve. So, when you draw up your goals that will get your ODD child their tokens, make sure that there is one easily attainable goal and some intermediate goals hidden in between. Depending on your child's age, it's also a good idea to consider how many behaviors you want to include in your system at one time based on whether your child will find a system with several behaviors or activities confusing or not.

- This point is just a reminder to remember the number one most important requirement when dealing with an ODD child, which is positivity. As with every other aspect, this system needs to be approached in a positive way, and the "difficult" goals should not be framed as reprehensible or repugnant behavior. Your child's behavior indicates in itself the amount of negativity they experience within themselves, so the more you can envelop them with positivity, the better. Help them to interpret these behaviors as aspects that can be improved, but not as traits they have because they are bad individuals. Every goal in the token economy system is equal in its value; however, you may consider implementing your own interpretation of the rewards regarding how much effort the child needs to put in to achieve it. Also note that, if you want to use the effort component to create tokens of different values, the concept of effort needs to be logically quantifiable. An incorrect way of interpreting the effort here would be to say that Annie worked "twice as hard," so she gets a token with a higher value. Avoid any abstract ideas when it comes to calculating and estimating rewards and tokens as children have a hard time understanding these abstract concepts.

- When a child earns a token, be present to hand it over in a congratulatory fashion. If you're going to handle this part of the process by telling your child, "Go get your token; it's on top of the fridge," there's an important element missing; the element where you physically acknowledge your child's achievement, which is vital to the systematic improvement of their behavior.

- Some other useful ideas are to help your child identify a special designated token container. This will work especially well with younger children as it will make the whole idea even more official and legitimate. You can go all out and decorate a jar or a container, stick on a label, and place it in a spot in the house where everyone can see it or in your child's room if they prefer it to be there.

- Choose a type of token that your child cannot find anywhere in the home and secretly add their own to the token jar. If you were to use marbles as tokens, your child may likely be able to source some marbles from a friend and secretly add them to the token jar. Now, we're not saying they'll do this, but you know kids. A good example of a token you can use is poker chips. You can also make your own tokens; just make sure that your child doesn't have access to them.

- If you want your token economy system to veer away from a materialistic venture, you can focus on coming up with rewards that don't cost money or that are not based on monetary status. For example, giving your child the newest PlayStation as a reward is likely going to create the impression that they'll expect something even bigger next time. Keep this in mind when you think about which rewards you want to give your children. The rewards can also teach them a lot about life and that not everything is about money. However, you still want them to enjoy the rewards, otherwise, the whole token economy idea may collapse.

- Although a token economy system is generally very successful when used with ODD children and teens, you may encounter a few bumps in the beginning. You can prepare yourself for the most common token economy system issues beforehand so you'll be ready to fix them if they should occur. One of the issues that you may have been thinking about while reading this discussion is that your child may not be interested in earning any tokens because they don't like the rewards that are being offered. If this is the case, you can consider discussing the rewards with your child and reaching a compromise that doesn't cross any of your boundaries, which could be a specific amount of money you're prepared to spend or something you are prepared to do. It may also be hard for your child to get the feel of the token economy system if they have a lot of privileges and are used to getting the things they ask for. Try using these privileges, for example, allowing them to play video games, as rewards.

- If you have more than one child, don't exclude the others from the token reward economy system. You can create some healthy competition and relationship-building by advertising the system as a positive way for your kids to work together and to give each child an easy, intermediate, and difficult goal to achieve. There can even be challenges where your kids need to work together in order to get their tokens, and you can call it a "group challenge."

- Finally, depending on what is available to you and what you've already made available to your child, try to provide a variety of rewards throughout the weeks as children can get bored easily. You can help them manage their "reward wealth" by using the tokens now for smaller rewards or by giving them bigger rewards that they will have to save up for, which means long-term good behavior

Establish Clear-Cut Rules

Rules are probably the things your ODD child loves complaining and arguing about the most because they become a convenient platform for an argument or a tantrum. They are usually also very vigilant when it comes to parents setting out the rules — if there's a loophole somewhere, they'll find it, and you will know the second they think something is unfair. So, this is a component that is separate from any rewards system you decide to implement in your house; this is about setting the ground rules. To avoid any "you said, they said" situations, create a rule card or document that clearly sets out all the rules, and stick it against the fridge or the back door where the whole family can see it.

If you want the rule list to be effective, don't make it too long, always refer to it with respect and refer to a family member who broke the rules with respect, and include basic rules that include chores, schoolwork, and family communication. Finally, make sure not to break any of the rules yourself and then be dismissive about it — this would ultimately destroy any attempt at getting your ODD child to understand why they have to follow the rules.

Don't Fall for Power Struggle Provocation

If you have an ODD child or teen, you know that your authority is being tested regularly. Children and teenagers with ODD love to and are good at trapping authority figures in ongoing arguments or debates about what they may find to be unfair or troublesome. However, if you have a household with a solid rule system that applies to everyone, there is no need to entertain your ODD child or teen in such an extended argument about their interpretation of right and wrong. If you've discussed the house rules with the family, including all of your children, and the necessary questions were answered, then there's no need to respond to unproductive power struggles.

Here is an example of what you can do. If you give your ODD child or teen a clear instruction to, for example, wash the dishes, and they try to argue back, move on straight to the consequence set for that action if you are confident that your instruction was clear. Your child will start an argument with you about washing the dishes because that's going to delay them actually having to go to the kitchen and wash the dishes. Don't fall for this delay tactic; make sure that your child understands the instruction, and if they don't comply, remind them of the consequences before enforcing it.

The point here is not to force your child into doing things they don't want to do, but it is more about maintaining fair and reasonable household rules. Giving them negative attention is going to feed their reactive tendencies, so just ensure that they are reminded of the house rules and that it is enforced if they do not do their part. When it comes to effectively dealing with ODD, you have two best friends that will always have your back: positivity and consistency (Morin, 2020b).

Consistency, Consistency, Consistency

It can't be said enough. ODD children thrive on loopholes, inconsistent behavior from authority figures and even their peers, and taking a gap when they see one. Your system should be as watertight as Noah's ark; however, instead of its requirements being to hold out water for forty days and forty nights while meandering the great floods, yours need to hold tight until your child reaches their post-teen years. That's what I call running a tight ship.

While taking all of this into consideration, your ODD child is not the only component your life consists of and you do have other priorities, many of which have been discussed in earlier chapters. Slipping up is going to happen. Making mistakes is inevitable. If your child becomes aware of this, they are going to use it as a trigger to react and misbehave because, even though they've been systematically weaned off the toxic behavior through your positive and consistent approach, they still have a psychiatric disorder, and they are neurologically wired to act that way. Don't let it get to you. Nip it in the bud by going on exactly the way you did before it happened. People make mistakes, but unfortunately, your child is not in a position to understand that yet.

Calm Down Your ODD Child

In most cases, when an ODD child or teen is on the verge of doing something aggressive or losing it completely, we counter this negative behavior with a negative word like "no" or "don't" or even a phrase like "stop that." At this point, the child is so sensitive to their own emotional instability that countering their behavior with a word like 'no' can send them over the edge. For most of us, the word no is negative, yes, but if someone tells us 'No,' we'll likely comply and not be triggered by its negative nature. Well, not an ODD child or teen. As with many scenarios we've discussed in this book, parents try their best to prevent and help, but their methods just seem to fuel the flames exactly because of these small details we overlook. I don't think anyone will deny that ODD resembles rebellious behavior, only it is much more complicated. And, what happens if you say no, don't, or "stop" to a rebellious individual? You can expect the opposite reaction.

Here's a technique that's going to make you giggle. Hopefully, your child will also giggle because that's the point! Try using a code word instead of words that communicate negative reinforcement like 'no' and the other ones we discussed earlier. You can either choose a word without discussing it with your child, or you can choose a word together so your child can use the word as well to warn you when they're about to have an episode. Imagine noticing that your child is blowing up and getting red in the face because they have to take out the trash and you just look at them and say 'swigglypoo' instead of using negative language. Their jaws just might drop to the floor. This can be your code word for all words that indicate negative reinforcement. When you see that mouth opening in protest... "remember dear, swigglypoo." Or, "But mom..." "I said, SWIG-GLY-POOOOOO." They'll know what it means in no time.

Alternatively, you and your ODD child or teen can work together by choosing a code word, and your child can let you know when they are feeling an aggressive episode coming. This will require a discussion with your child, which can also be a positive experience for them. You can empower your child by allowing them to choose the word, and then you can talk about what should happen if they give you the code word. For example, should you go for a quick walk around the block? Or, maybe you should go and shoot some hoops. I would just put on some loud music and start dancing like a crazy person to make my child laugh. Soon enough, they'll be dancing with you.

Work With your Child's Teachers and School

If your child is not being homeschooled by yours truly or your partner, you need to discuss your child's condition with their teacher or teachers, and any other individuals who may need to be aware of the possible complications it can cause. This is because, when it comes to learning, an ODD child is most often a special needs child, especially if they have co-occurring conditions that involve ADHD, or language learning or cognition issues. For example, whether your child is attending school online or going to school, you can ask the teacher to remove any distracting items in the background of the online classroom like multicolored posters. Alternatively, if your child will be sitting in an actual classroom, you can ask the teacher to seat them in the front, where they won't be able to see so much movement from the students behind them.

Another example of something small that can make a big difference in an ODD child's behavior is making class activities very structured, and it will work extremely well if the teacher can provide a large planner on the wall in a physical classroom where all the students can see it or a digital one the teacher and your child has access to in an online setting, which indicates when they are going to do what during class. This structural addition is very important and can spare you a lot of arguments and conflict in the classroom setting.

It may be hard to discuss all these requirements with your child's teacher, but they may not have dealt with an ODD child before, and while it may seem to them that you want to change their teaching style, most of the information you provide them is to make their day as conflict-free as possible. It's crucial for them to understand this because, if they don't and they find your approach a bit overbearing, they may consider ignoring your advice altogether, which they will regret for a long time. I decided to mention this now because the next aspect you may want to discuss with a teacher is how they communicate with the students. Instead of providing information and expecting the students to accept it for what it is, it is much more prudent to follow an approach where you engage them in the discussion, especially if there's an opinionated ODD student present. By following this approach, the teacher gives the ODD child an opportunity for a healthy release, which lessens the chance of a buildup and subsequent explosion later. The next suggestion is for the teacher to include a program or lessons about emotional regulation that actively focuses on teaching children how to handle powerful emotions like anger and frustration. This can be easily organized if your child is attending school online; however, if that is not the case, you may have to organize a meeting with the school staff. You can also enquire about bullying and well-being programs that teach children how to be resilient when they have to face tough situations like these.

Finally, it is very important for the teacher or teachers to understand the required balance between rewards versus punishment. It's pointless if you as the parent, have a great and healthy system going home, but your child's teachers at school do not focus on rewarding your child at all because they are only focusing on their bad behavior. It's like building up your child and sending them to school just to be broken down again. Always make sure that, whether your child attends school in an online setting or physical setting, the teacher has a profound understanding of how important positive reinforcement is for the well-being of your child (raisingchildren.net.au, 2020).

Empower the Siblings

If your ODD child or teen has siblings, they are probably dealing with the same stress and aggression you are. Having an ODD child and other children is going to require you to not only divide your focus but also turn each eye into a super-powered laser beam, at least at the beginning when a system has not been established yet and your household is relatively chaotic.

Why it's Difficult

The nature of the relationships between ODD children and teens and their siblings resembles a constant power struggle because your ODD child is on a constant mission to control everything. Sharing, considering another's wants and needs, and playing nice are not ideas that likely exist in their minds, and these concepts will have to be planted and cultivated with care and patience. Meanwhile, you have to look after the well-being of your other children, and it is important for them to understand the situation without retaliating in a confrontational situation by bullying your ODD child due to their condition.

Siblings may react in ways like these because of the high levels of stress and frustration they have to deal with. As parents, we can all understand that this is not a healthy environment for them, and it can cause feelings of resentment if they feel that their ODD sibling gets away with misbehavior without being properly punished. They may feel neglected and become rebellious against how the household is being run because of the hurt and anger they are experiencing. A common strategy that parents use when children fight is to let them sort out their issues or differences on their own. However, this is not a prudent strategy when one of the siblings has ODD. Because they take conflict and aggressive behavior to a completely new level and have no interest in sorting out the issue, your intervention is crucial.

Teach Them to Look for Signs

One strategy you can teach your affected siblings is to identify the warning signs and shut down the communication completely and leave their ODD sibling alone. For example, you can ask your child, "have you noticed what your brother does before he throws a tantrum?" Your child may say, "Yes, he balls his fists and he gets red in the face." If you can see that your child has identified these warning signs, tell them to just turn around and walk away. Tell them, "I know it's hard because your brother's anger frustrates you, but if you just turn around and walk away, he has nobody to fight with." Avoid saying something like, "If you turn around and walk away, you'll be the better person." This will give your child the wrong idea, and the way you want to show your children that they are also important is not to use language that suggests you favor them over your ODD child or teen.

Empower Them with Choices

Another important message your children need to hear from you is that it's okay for them to set boundaries and to recognize and respect the boundaries of other family members. They can claim their own emotional and physical space, and they can inform another family member if they've entered that space without their approval. Your children need to hear this from you as their parent because their ODD sibling is only aware of their own boundaries and not anyone else's. This is a way to empower your children by telling them that they also have a rightful place in the household, but they still need to deal with an invasion of space or a crossing of boundaries in a non-confrontational way. This should not be a reason for them to fight with their ODD sibling.

Redress

The implementation of fair restitution by you will mean a lot to your affected siblings. In a household with an ODD child, making fairness a priority will help the siblings to feel worthy, experience fewer feelings of resentment, and give them a feeling of belonging. This implementation of redress is, of course, meant to go both ways, and your children should understand that. So, if one of your siblings is in the wrong, restitution will be applied the same way it would have if the culprit was their ODD sibling. This should be done in an almost stoic fashion, where emotions do not rule the actions taken in such a situation, but rather the actions themselves. For example, the restitution or redress should not be done with an air of "oh, it's you this time, is it?" Turn your face into a blank slate that is unreadable so your children can shift their focus to your actions. If you do this the first few times, there may be some bombs exploding in your house. Just keep that consistency going. You show your child that you love them, so no guilty feelings are allowed!

Praise Initiative

When you start implementing new rules in your household, chances are you are going to experience a lot of resistance and possibly aggression. However, there is also a chance that your children may develop the ability to solve problems on their own that could've ended up in conflict situations, especially if you expose them to a positive and proactive environment at home. These attempts and successes should be celebrated as they are an indication of growth, especially if they involve communication between your ODD child or teen and a sibling. Praise their efforts and always help them to understand how it contributes to your family's goal of being a cohesive and loving unit (Abraham & Studaker, 2020).

Chapter 7. Building Your Child's Self-Esteem

A person's self-esteem can be described as how much they value themselves and their self-worth in their world. Building your child's self-esteem is crucial because a positive self-image makes them feel good about themselves.

Children with positive self-esteem feel self-assured and proficient. They see their own self-worth and believe in their capabilities. They find satisfaction in the things they manage to do themselves and will always put in major effort to achieve their best.

When children are self-assured about who they are, they'll have a higher probability to have an open-minded mentality and they will encourage themselves to undertake new tasks while managing and learning from their slip-ups. They are confident in their ability to stand up for themselves and will seek aid from their guardians when necessary.

Children with a positive self-esteem

- Feel appreciated

- Are tough and feel satisfied when they know they did their best

- Have self-control

- Are self-reliant

- Believe in themselves

- Are proud

Children with negative self-esteem:

- Feel unsatisfied, irritated, anxious, or unhappy

- Fears of failure

- Lacks confidence

- Self-doubt

- Feelings of inferiority

How is Self-esteem Developed?

Children develop positive self-esteem by achieving their goals and realizing that hard work has its rewards.

Achieving things in life demonstrates to them that they have what it takes to fulfill their dreams and future aspirations. Their little victories give them positive affirmation, and they acquire the mindset that as long as they give their best, it's more than good enough, even if they fail.

When children accomplish things, it delights other people, like their friends and families who they care about. These positive reactions also make them feel good and over time, they begin to build confidence and great self-esteem.

Children with low self-esteem are prone to failure and don't get a great deal of positive feedback from others. As a result, they feel unsure of themselves and their own abilities. They could start to lack motivation and give up trying to do things because of their fear of failure. They find it difficult to deal with any mistakes they make and deep down, they may not accept the fact that they're worthy to succeed.

The 4-Step Plan to Help Develop Your Child's Self-Esteem

Children with ODD already struggle with so many behavioral issues and things like rejection, loneliness, and probably low self-esteem.

As parents, you need to help develop self-assurance and confidence by finding those little things that your child is actually good at. Developing a solid emotional bond, and rewarding your child when you notice their determination even if they did not succeed, will help build a positive self-image over time.

Each kid is born with talents, some have many and others have one exceptional gift, but we all have them. Even a child with ODD has astonishing abilities, but it might be more difficult to find them because they remain concealed, even when they are uncovered, your child might find it difficult to share with the rest of the world. I am going to share 4 secrets on how you can develop your child's self-esteem and allow them to become who they are supposed to become.

Your child needs to know from day one that you love them unconditionally. They are going to get so much negative attention outside in the real world when they get older, so now is the time for you to build their feelings of self-worth and belonging.

Before they become another statistic or are categorized as bad or naughty, you need to focus on their positive traits. Don't pay much attention to the pathologists. They have to put a child with a certain disorder into a box or a certain category so they fail to recognize the intricacies, the deep emotional connections, and the essence of your ODD child's soul.

Many kids lose their individuality when they are branded as a child with a mental or behavioral condition. Read these four steps to help your child have positive self-esteem and try to ascend past the ODD label's limits.

Develop and Build Connections

Connecting with our children is just as important to us parents as it is to our kids. When our children believe that we love them and our bond is strong, we are guaranteed to have a healthy relationship. We need to remember that they look to us for guidance, they need a constant in their lives and the only way to retain a strong bond with our kids is through daily habits of connection.

Give them love and physical attention. A good morning kiss or a goodbye hug. Happiness in the house should be a daily tradition that gives your kid the opportunity to laugh even over their mistakes or disappointments that could cause a disconnect if not dealt with appropriately.

Switch off your phone and ask your kid to take a break from their technological gadgets to enjoy each other's company and have some family time. Communicate, relate to one another, debate or argue, even if you don't see eye to eye make sure you connect. Go on family excursions together or just go for a walk on the beach. Showing your ODD child how to bond and build healthy connections will ensure that they don't go through life isolated and alone.

The Importance of Play

Play is an important part of every youngster's healthy development. It advances crucial life skills, such as self-assurance and individuality. Play is a safe place to rehearse executive decision-making and develops self-confidence. Playtime allows your child to accomplish their own goals, eventually enhancing their self-assurance.

During playtime, children make up their own rules. It allows them the freedom to choose what they want to do and expands their executive skills. They become more self-assured as they are given further occasions to make their own choices.

Encouraging your youngsters to resolve their own problems during play permits them to seek out more play-based learning strategies on their own. Although it is good to challenge and inspire kids during play, we must also give them the chance to discover things on their own.

Boost Problem Solving Skills

As soon as your child begins to develop general problem-solving skills in their daily life, they will realize that they can resolve challenges and difficulties on their own. Once they develop the confidence, they need to tackle the next activity that is challenging and significant to them; they are on the road to success. Each kid can conquer any type of situation, as long as they receive reassurance and guidance from their parents or caregivers. Remember the only thing that matters is improvement and progress, not perfection.

Give Praise

We all know how vital it is to commend our children when they achieved something they worked hard at. Self-esteem develops over time when kids put in the effort to reach certain goals and feel good about them when they achieve them. What you say as a parent and how you say it will help your child to recognize things that they should be proud of. Praise also helps build a strong bond between the child and the parent or caregiver. Achieving goals is important, but you shouldn't just solely focus on your child's accomplishments. You need to take your child's feelings into account as well. If they accomplish numerous goals, but they are unhappy or living a detached, miserable childhood, their accomplishments mean nothing to them.

Rather, make sure you raise a content child with confidence, self-assurance, passion, sociability, and ethical righteousness. This will ensure their future is bright regardless of their educational triumphs.

Vanquishing Your Child's Low Self-Esteem

Every child and especially kids diagnosed with ODD needs a sense of social and academic success, as well as the reassurance of your unconditional love regardless of the triumphs or failures in their life.

Being incessantly corrected and continually disciplined, most kids with ODD or other learning disabilities regularly develop low self-esteem. They start to think that they're just a failure and will never be clever enough. We certainly know that these feelings of being disappointed are far from accurate, but we need to support our youngsters and highlight their strong points so we can build up their self-confidence.

Adverse Responses

Everybody has a limit. A time when they just had enough and responded to a situation in a negative manner without thinking before they speak. Children with ODD can drive their parents up the wall with their defiance and bad behavior, and sometimes we feel so angry that we shout at them or say something that makes us feel so guilty afterward. We might even dodge our kids entirely.

We need to think about why we struggle to talk to them in a peaceful and loving way. Could it be because your youngster's restless, inattentiveness, or impetuous actions are too overbearing, and if so, is their ODD being treated adequately?

How are they performing at school? Could they maybe have undiagnosed educational problems? If your kid's ODD behavior is causing adverse responses from you, other relatives, or peers, it's crucial that you contemplate the influence this has on his self-worth.

George's Story:

George, a child suffering from both ADHD and ODD, was exhibiting alarming behavioral and psychological issues at home and at school. His parents did not believe in medication or any behavioral tactics from an experienced professional. His teacher suggested that he goes for a mental assessment and after the necessary evaluations, George was diagnosed with ADHD and ODD. Once he was put on the correct medication combined with the appropriate behavioral methods to treat his ODD, George started to show great progress at school and at home. Sometimes, he would still display behavioral difficulties. It was then discovered that his parents would shout at him or give snide remarks when he did something wrong. After going for family therapy both parents realized that the way they communicated with him was not only affecting his self-esteem, it also made him feel like a failure. They have since adjusted their attitudes and the way they communicated with one another, and now the family is showing great feats of success.

Achievements at School

Most children who suffer from ODD have difficulties at school. Their teachers might see them as disobedient and disruptive because they were not informed of your child's disorder. Have an appropriate discussion with your child's educator about their condition. They might be struggling with things like their attentiveness, or participating during a lesson. They might get angry or aggressive because they struggle with their schoolwork overall.

Ask the teacher for feedback about any behavioral complications your child might be exhibiting and explain how a difference in the educator's approach might help. Maybe all your kid requires is improved management during school breaks and in-between classes. They might only need slight assistance to refocus when they begin to daydream. A learning disability doesn't mean the child will never be able to succeed at school, it just means they need a bit more attention from their educators than the average student.

If your child is taking medication, maybe consult your doctor about alternative medications that could help with their issues at school, or talk to your psychologist about additional therapy options to improve their awareness and boost concentration.

The Significance of Relationships with Peers

Effective education is one aspect to focus on. Relationships with peers is another important area you need to help your child with. Kids with ODD find it very difficult to make a connection with a fellow classmate.

Keep an eye on your kid when they ask a friend over to play. Pay attention to their actions. For example, are they nervous and worried about participating in any games with their friends? Do they have difficulty understanding social cues from their peers? Do they become too preoccupied, impetuous, or hyper to play with others? Do they try to elude any type of physical activity because of inadequate gross motor skills like kicking a ball? Can they understand the essence of being part of a team? Do they lack the ability to concentrate when playing board games?

As soon as you have an idea of your ODD kid's exact social difficulties, you can begin to search for resolutions. They might have to go for additional treatment or attempt a physical activity that they don't need to be physically apt in some areas.

Building positive self-esteem takes effort, but when you notice your child's smile when they start participating and mingling with their peers, you will realize that everything was worth it.

Using Active Praise to Build Your Child's Self-Esteem

You will be surprised how you can develop your child's self-esteem by praising their positive behavior regardless of how minor they are. When you emphasize your delight when you notice positive behavior, you inspire your child to continue their good behavior instead of falling back into negative patterns. Just a few words of encouragement will build your child's self-confidence, diminish their negative behavior, and reinforce that vital emotional bond between you two.

It might sound so simple to just say a couple of reassuring words when your child is being good, but what if your child has ODD and you only notice all their bad behaviors? Our automatic response is to scold or reprimand our kids because we feel it is the only way they will recognize their mistakes and learn not to repeat these errors. The problem is when we only concentrate on the negatives, we are actually increasing the chances that their undesirable behaviors will continue, which will ultimately harm that already fragile emotional bond.

The trick with an ODD child is to find even the tiniest positive behavior and focus on that. Praise tells your child that you noticed their good behavior and that you expressed your delight. Descriptive praise is not the same as usual praise. With descriptive or effective praise, you don't just tell your child that you are happy because they behaved, you need to explain to your child precisely what actions made you happy and why it's important for them to continue with this behavior. Kids need detailed direction. Descriptive praise, tells your child exactly what is expected from them and decreases uncertainty or misunderstanding.

A few examples of using effective or descriptive praise include:

Finding Something Positive

If your child is throwing a tantrum or being aggressive, it might feel impossible to find something good to focus on. Instead of telling them what not to do, you can tell them how pleased you are that they did not act out on their aggression by becoming physical.

Specify the Positive Behavior You Want Them to Repeat

If we use the above-mentioned example, we can tell our children that they must remember it is never the right thing to do to harm others. Explain to them that if they are unhappy or angry about something, they should rather come and tell you why they feel that way so you can figure out what to do together.

Motivate Your Child to Behave Positively

Telling your child that not being aggressive makes you happy will not motivate them to stop. Instead, explain to them that they will lose privileges like TV time if they do hurt anyone, they have a reason not to do it. If they do turn to violence instead of coming to you as you asked, you have to stick to the consequence you mentioned. So, because they hurt someone, their television privilege will be revoked.

Reward Good Behavior

Rewarding your child for positive behaviors is a brilliant way to emphasize productive conduct. It does not have to be a toy or ice cream or chocolates either, you can give them additional TV time or five minutes longer when riding their bike outside or even choosing a family activity over the weekend. You will quickly realize that when you begin finding positive aspects in your child's behavior, they will start recognizing these traits in others and soon the entire family will use effective praise.

Strengthening Self-Esteem in Kids with Concentration Difficulties

Children who suffer from behavioral and psychological disorders find it very difficult to focus. They are impulsive, struggle with authority figures, and become defiant when expected to follow rules. This can make things very difficult for educators. Giving consequences or threatening kids with expulsion will only produce feelings of insufficiency and embarrassment. To get an ODD child who lacks the focus to thrive, you need to explain to them that you are pleased with their determination even though they get sidetracked easily. To help them cope with feelings of irritation, hopelessness, or uncertainty that regularly go together with concentration difficulties, you can make use of some of these approaches:

Find the Root of the Matter

When your child is exhibiting aggression or frustration it is not because they are deliberately being naughty, instead, chances are that they feel

89

overwhelmed about something that they are struggling to achieve or handle. Your job is to focus on the reason behind their behavior. If they don't understand certain parts of their homework or if a school project is just too difficult to finish, you can help.

As soon as you find the issues behind their reaction you can discuss them with your child's educator to help break down the overpowering school material.

Break Major Problems into Manageable Parts

How do you deal with one massive problem? You break it into smaller, more manageable pieces. An ODD child struggles to focus, so help them by breaking a large project into a sequence of minor endeavors. Children might require a parent or educator to support them and offer some kind of framework for them to follow. Help them with one question for example and then tell them that you will be close to assist if they need you, but they must try to resolve the rest of the problems on their own. Staying calm when working with your ODD child on their problem regularly has a reassuring influence on them, and they will try harder to conquer their schoolwork or projects.

Checklists Work

Most of us have a diary that we use to keep track of our day. Get your child to write a comprehensive to-do list. It helps them feel like they accomplished that specific task when they can mark it has done or fulfilled.

Remain Hands-on and Communicate

Preoccupied kids generally freeze when they come across difficulties in their schoolwork. You need to be proactive and remain involved with both their homework and their educators to ensure there is always someone to help them when they need it.

Empower but Never Enable

Kids who have trouble focusing often feel like they can never succeed on their own. As a parent, we overcompensate by doing their homework or projects for them, but this just solidifies their feeling of failure. Tell your child that you are confident that if they try, you know they will do well.

Stay In the Now

Children with low concentration levels already struggle with racing thoughts. Promising them a reward in the near future will not encourage them to work harder. They need something tangible to hold onto now. Rather tell them that as soon as you two finished with the schoolwork you can go for ice cream. This will motivate them to do their best in the present moment.

Use Previous Victories

When your child is becoming agitated because they are struggling with something, try to remind them of a previous situation when they did achieve their goals. Ask them to think about which tactics they utilized to succeed then and to see which strategies they can apply to this specific problem.

Intervene Before They React

As soon as you notice the beginnings of a temper tantrum intercede before it turns into a massive drama. Look for the telltale signs or body language that shows they are becoming irritated so you can calm them down before they lose control.

Remain Calm and Stable

Never raise your voice, regardless of how frustrated you might be. Yelling makes your child more jittery and on edge. Rather try to explain your expectations in a gentle way instead of trying to control the situation. A calm approach always works wonders.

Show Empathy

Kids who are easily distracted already feel insufficient at everything they do. These children need additional consideration, inspiration, and understanding. Show compassion and try to help your child remain motivated. Many times, all your kid needs are an empathetic ear to listen to make them feel better about themselves.

Boosting your child's self-esteem can help them cope with mistakes that they might make and helps them feel proud and independent.

Chapter 8. The 9-Step Positive Parenting Plan

As parents, you always want what's best for your child, no matter what. But sometimes, we forget to see our kids' eye-to-eye, trying to understand what they are going through. Sometimes, your hectic schedule catches up to you and you find yourself on the proverbial "short end" of the parenting stick, with your patience thinning out.

In such scenarios, it is always important to remember that you are your child's guide, and your behavior can later reflect on them.

But given that the dynamic of your interactions with your child can shift quickly, it is always better to be mindful of certain things. After all, the path to improvement in your child's behavior starts with you.

Proper Parental Traits

We all want to raise a healthy, happy child, but many of us wonder: how do I approach my role as a parent? Do I just go with the flow, or do I use similar parenting methods my parents used?

Regardless of what your parenting style or your parenting concerns may be, you need to help foster understanding, morality, independence, self-discipline, compassion, collaboration, and joyfulness in your child. Here are a few parenting traits to keep in mind to ensure you encourage your child and help them achieve their life goals.

Lead and Support, Don't Force or Demand

Parents should never force a child to do anything under any circumstances, even if you think you are only pushing them a little bit to achieve their best; they will probably do the exact opposite and will likely quit altogether. You can never give a child too much love or support; show them that they can lean on you when things get difficult and that they have a confidant in you.

Discipline is Key

Create and set rules. A child will struggle to learn self-efficacy if you do not manage their behavior when they are young. The rules your child learns at home will form the rules they apply to themselves later in life. Remember there is a difference between discipline and punishment. Kids who lack discipline are usually unappreciative, materialistic, and will have difficulties making friends and being content when they reach adulthood.

Children Absorb Everything

It doesn't matter if it's bad language, inappropriate behavior, or the way you treat others, your child watches you and will emulate your every move. Remember every action has a reaction, so before doing anything at the spur of the moment, think about the results. Always be on your best behavior to teach your kids respect and empathy.

Never Be Nasty, Vindictive, or Hostile

Everybody can get irritated or annoyed, it's normal, but as soon as we become abusive or degrade others, we teach our children that it is OK to be condescending and mean. It is important to teach your child that they must treat others the way they would like to be treated.

Where, Who, What

As a parent, you need to know: Where your child is, who the child is with, and what they are doing. Don't feel like you are micromanaging your child by asking these questions, you have to ensure they are safe and stay out of harm's way, regardless of their age. Their job is to learn, have fun, and enjoy their childhood. Your job is to make sure that they do just that.

Foster Independence

Of course, you need to have rules and set some limits in order for your child to learn self-control, but you also need to encourage them to be independent so they can learn a sense of self-direction. True success in life is finding a balance between the two. It's ordinary for kids to drive for self-sufficiency, and children will push for their own independence because it is part of their human nature to want to feel in control of their lives. Keep in mind that it is fine to assist your child with something if you are educating them to ultimately do it on their own.

Show Them Love

Make time for your children, ask them how their day was, and actually listen to them. Even if it's a five-minute conversation in the car after school, as long as you keep on strengthening that bond between you and as long as they feel they are truly loved, that is the only thing that matters.

Recognize Your Child for Who They Are

Live in the here and now, see your child in this present moment, not what they will become in the future. It is normal for parents to only want what's best for their kids. To make sure their children have everything they never had, but remember your child is an individual, they might love activities you despised. So don't push them to take part in events they don't want to. You can suggest that they try something to see if they might like it, but never live your life and your unrealized dreams through them.

Be There and Talk, Talk, Talk

Being involved in your child's life and being a hands-on parent does take time and effort, and it regularly means reconsidering and reorganizing your priorities. You might have to sacrifice your own needs for your child's requests, but if you are there mentally, emotionally, and physically, you'll be astonished by the connection you build with your child and will learn things about your child you never knew. Don't stop talking and don't stop listening to one another. Don't just talk to your child, have a conversation with them.

Teach Respect

If you treat your child with respect, they will learn to respect others. Explain to your child that they need to give everybody the same consideration, love, empathy, and charity they expect in return. Speaking to them about gratitude and always remembering who they are as a person is way more significant than what they will achieve.

9 Steps to Parent a Child with ODD

Enhance your ODD Child's Self-esteem

Infants develop their own personalities as they grow, but as babies, they perceive the world and themselves through their parents' viewpoints, as well as their behaviors. Many kids copy the mannerisms, expressions, and even the way their parents talk. Everything you say and do as a parent will influence the development of your children's self-image. Always praise your kids for even the smallest triumph so they can build confidence and pride. Allowing them to accomplish things on their own will build their independence and show them that they have the capability to achieve anything they want to. Never be condescending and don't compare your child with anybody else. This will increase their feelings of insignificance.

Negative statements or remarks like "You can be so stupid sometimes!" or "You are such a spoilt brat!" can hurt more than any physical injury.

Think before you speak and be empathetic when your child makes a mistake. Explain to them that everybody has slip-ups and that even though you do not agree with their behavior, you will always love them.

Make Time for Your Kids

These days we as parents are so busy with work and life that we don't have the luxury to spend hours with our kids. It doesn't mean that we are bad parents, it just means that we need to prioritize the time we have appropriately. Spending quality time with our children is critical if we want to raise them to become well-rounded, happy individuals.

Quality time doesn't mean a great road trip or an expensive activity. You can have a wonderful time eating dinner together, playing a board game, or just building a puzzle. Getting a movie that they love and letting them help you make some snacks to eat while watching it together is a fantastic way to bond. Even helping with homework opens up opportunities to spend time together and to bond.

Kids who don't get attention from their parents need to regularly overreact and misbehave; just to get your attention. Remember any attention is better than none, so negative attention will do.

Regardless of your busy schedule, make sure that you spend some quality time with your child every day to talk, bond, and get to know one another.

Recognize Positive Behavior

Reduce the number of times you react negatively and harshly to your kids on a given day. Ensure you do not criticize them too much. Instead, compliment them more often to increase their self-esteem.

Make an effort to find something to compliment every day. Please give them a hug or a kiss after the compliment. After a while, you'll realize that you're encouraging the kinds of behaviors you want to see in your home.

Sometimes we don't realize our antagonistic responses towards our kids. We might disapprove of most of their actions instead of applauding their good behaviors. Even if we have the best intentions, our continuous scolding might give our kids the impression that we are their supervisor instead of their parents. Identify and praise every positive action you notice and remind your kids how much you love and appreciate them. Mentioning all their good traits will encourage your child to do their level best in everything they do. Compliments, rewards, and acts of love are vital for effective parenting and better behavior from your ODD child.

Be a Good Role Model

You will be surprised how your behavior rubs off on your child. Kids assume the behavior of their parents is acceptable. So, before responding in an aggressive manner in front of your kids, think twice about the fact that your child will respond in a similar way when they get mad. Children who imitate aggression usually have a parent or role model who displays this kind of behavior at home.

The best approach to be an effective parent is to model appropriate behavior. If you model appropriate behavior your children will follow. Always be truthful, approachable, humble, caring, and gentle. Remember you need to treat your kids the same way you would like to be treated.

Be Consistent With Your Discipline

As a parent, you need to set limits and restrictions to teach discipline. The core objective of disciplining your children is to imprint qualities of self-control into their character while helping them to distinguish between acceptable and offensive behaviors in public. Occasionally, your children will test the limits you put in place, but as long as you make sure that you set restrictions that have consequences when broken, they will soon realize that you mean business. Begin with a warning, then time out, followed by taking away an activity they enjoy, such as playing games. Consistent consequences also ensure that your child knows what to expect when they don't follow the rules you set out for them.

Fine-tune Your Parenting Style

As a parent, you have a major influence on everything your child does and thinks. Every parent has their own parenting style which can be explained as the approach you take to communicate with your child, as well as how you discipline them. Parenting styles change through the years as your child changes. There are four main parenting styles, and we will briefly explain each one.

The Permissive Parent:

These types of parents can be identified as too soft. They might say that they will hand out consequences for bad behavior but usually never follow through. They will only really get involved when the child is extremely disobedient. They're quite lenient and kids with ODD can persuade them to take back any consequences given easily.

The Uninvolved Parent:

The uninvolved parent has no idea or minimal information about their kid's movements, their friends, and their whereabouts. These parents have limited rules if any, and their kids remain unsupervised without any guidance.

The Authoritarian Parent:

The emphasis for an authoritarian parent is on strict rules and total compliance. They are not interested in communication with their kids and want children to do, as they say, no exceptions.

Of all the parental styles mentioned, this approach is the best. Authoritative parents have rules and consequences but listen to their child's opinions, putting their child's feelings first while staying in charge.

Authoritative parents are devoted to their kids, putting in the time and effort to ensure bad behavioral complications are stopped before they become uncontrollable. They also use constructive discipline approaches to strengthen positive behavior in their child. Thus, raising happy, accountable, efficient kids who have no problem sticking to positive choices and avoiding dangerous situations.

We know ODD kids can be challenging but if you remain diligent, loving, and apply the proper type of discipline, you will notice tiny, subtle changes.

Always Communicate Properly

Remember that old saying, don't just hear someone, listen to them? You need to actually listen to your child to help them learn and develop good communication skills as well as healthy, strong family connections. Communicating with your kid in a positive manner will build positive self-esteem because they will feel that their opinion is valued. Positive open communication allows your kid to talk to you when any challenging conditions happen in their life. Kids have their own opinions as well as valid points, and they deserve proper explanations if they ask for one. Be open and honest about your expectations. If there is a problem, define it, tell them how you feel about it, and ask your child for suggestions to help find a solution.

Make sure you give consequences for bad behavior, but first listen to their side of the story. Imagine your child did something wrong if they know that they can come to you with an issue, knowing that you will understand their reason for doing something if they tell you the truth, your child will come to you directly when they need guidance and support. Negotiation is also vital. Children who feel part of a decision are more determined to stick to them. So, figure out appropriate consequences for negative behavior together.

Confirm Your Love is Unconditional

As an authority figure, you are in control when it comes to the adjustment of your child's behavior, as well as guiding them in the right direction. The way that you achieve this is to show them, unconditional love, regardless of what they do. This does not mean that you don't give out consequences or never discipline them. It means when you do discuss their behavior, you never make them feel guilty or be too critical. Don't demoralize their self-worth, rather attempt to foster self-regulation and reassure them of your love. When you discipline them, take care to explain your disappointment in their actions, but never in them. Comfort them and explain that you will always love them regardless.

Distinguish Your Own Needs and Limits as a Parent

There is no such thing as a perfect human being, rather embrace your imperfections as a parent and work on the things you would like to change in both yourself as well as your defiant child.

Concentrate on the parts of your household that require the most dedication first and then tackle the rest of the issues separately. There is no shame in acknowledging when you're too overwhelmed. Take a break now and then to do something that brings you and your partner joy. Putting yourself first does not make you self-centered, it merely shows that you are human. Taking care of your own happiness is another vital lesson you can teach your kids.

Let's see how as a parent, you can change things in order to support your kids, one by one.

Chapter 9. Medication and Treatment, Different Types of Therapies

Medication: There are certain medications that children and adults with ODD can benefit from using in conjunction with PMT or when PMT isn't an option. The drugs that are used most commonly are mood stabilizers, antidepressants, anti-anxiety medications, stimulants, and antipsychotics. It should also be noted that these medications aren't always used on children and if they do, they need to be monitored by a doctor who is aware of the side effects and how the medication might interact with your child's body, mind, and/or personality. For children who have long-term behaviors that are bad enough to warrant a diagnosis of ODD, then the doctor will likely prescribe mood stabilizers, which are used to calm aggressive and impulsive behaviors.

You may want to discuss with your child's doctor whether or not it's a good idea for them to take medications for ODD as well as PMT. The doctor may think that since your child is only young that it might not be a good idea for them to use medications, but many children who use PMT also need the assistance of medications in order to see improvement in their behavior. Sometimes parents will try to find their own methods for ODD treatment and although these methods may have worked for other children of their age, it may not be the best idea for your child to use them.

ODD Treatment

ODD, like other mental and mood disorders, is treatable, and there is such a wide variety of treatments one can choose from that you may not know where to start. Additionally, applying the "let's start at one point and go through all of them until we find one that works" approach can cause more harm than good, not only to your child or teen's mental state or condition but also to their self-esteem. Imagine jumping from treatment to treatment and being put under the impression that none of them are working on you? That would make me even more discontent and angry at the world, and it can give an ODD child or teen the opportunity to legitimize a reason to act the way they do.

There will be a trial-and-error component with all mental health treatments, but what you want to achieve is minimizing it to the extreme by firstly being informed and secondly, arming yourself with the most current knowledge available. Now that we've covered the nature, symptoms, manifestation, and coordinating disorders related to ODD, let's move on to the available treatments, what each type of treatment can offer your child or teen, how they are different and how they may be similar, and the reasons one would opt for a specific type of treatment in specific circumstances.

Why isn't ODD Curable?

Treatment can help you and your child manage oppositional defiant disorder, but there is currently no known cure for it. The reason why medical specialists don't know what the cure is or why it is not curable may be related to the fact that they are not completely sure and can't pinpoint an exact cause. The cause for ODD appears to consist of multiple factors, which include environmental, neurological, and even genetic components. Similar to the fact that researchers and medical practitioners know what the influential and contributing factors are that one can associate with an individual's potential to develop ODD, so are they also aware of therapeutic and psychiatric treatments that can subdue the symptoms, but not cure it completely.

The types of treatment for ODD are mostly psychological and in the form of psychotherapy, and some can be applied on their own while others can be used in conjunction with other treatments. Your child's treatment may also depend on whether they have a co-occurring condition, which may affect the approach or techniques required for effective treatment. Below is a discussion of the most common types of ODD treatment and how they work.

Types of ODD Treatment

If you are a parent with an ODD child or teen and you are currently looking for some type of treatment, rest assured that there are many different ways and methods to treat ODD. Speaking to a therapist and giving them the opportunity to get to know your child may also allow them to identify a type of treatment that will work best, which is better than randomly choosing one.

Cognitive Behavioral Therapy

Cognitive behavioral theory, also known as CBT, is characterized as a psychotherapeutic treatment that aims to help people learn how to first identify and then change disturbing or destructive patterns of thought that influence their behavior and emotions negatively. This means that cognitive behavioral therapy aims to change negative thoughts that occur automatically and that cause and can worsen emotional issues in a person's life, which can also be related to depression and anxiety. Studies have indicated that spontaneous negative and even harmful thoughts have a pernicious and unwanted influence on an individual's mood.

The most basic way to explain the CBT process is by identifying three steps during the therapy. First, the negative or harmful thoughts are identified, next, they are challenged by the individual who experienced them with the support of a therapist, and finally, they are to be replaced with thoughts that are more realistic and objective.

The idea behind or the philosophy of CBT is based on the identification of thought patterns. There is quite a wide range of strategies that are used in CBT to help individuals change their thought patterns. These may include role-playing, mental distractions, relaxation techniques, or journaling. Additionally, apart from the fact that there is a variety of techniques, there are also types of cognitive behavioral therapy that are important to be cognizant about. These 'types' are also directly related to the way they differ methodically, although still based on the same philosophy or principles. All the types involve relevant techniques that are aimed at addressing emotions, thoughts, and their subsequent behaviors, and each has a specific focus related to their difference in methodology.

As we mentioned, Cognitive therapy is based on identifying and altering distorted or unrealistic thinking patterns, which lead to related emotional responses and subsequent behaviors.

Dialectical behavior therapy or (DBT) also aims to address thoughts and their subsequent emotions and behaviors. However, it utilizes strategies that include mindfulness and emotional regulation.

Multimodal Therapy is a psychological method that requires one to address seven interconnected modalities when addressing thoughts and behavioral issues. These modalities are sensation, behavior, affect, imagery, cognition, interpersonal factors, and biological or drug considerations.

Rational emotive behavior therapy or REBT follows the process of first identifying irrational beliefs, actively challenging the beliefs identified, and then moving to a state of recognition and change to improve thought patterns.

After reading through all the types of CBT, one can see that, although they may take different methodical and therapeutic avenues, the goal remains the same. The nice thing about different types is that a specific approach or therapy type may be more compatible with a certain type of person than another. Although two different individuals may have the same disorder, there are more customized ways to approach and treat them.

CBT is usually used as a short-term treatment but has an astonishingly wide range of disorders that can effectively treat and improve the symptoms. The reason may be that all of these disorders are based on negative or irrational thought patterns. Examples of conditions that benefit from CBT are personality disorders, panic attacks, anxiety disorders, bipolar disorder, addictive behavior, anger problems, phobias, and stress control issues. During CBT, the therapist takes on an active role in the therapeutic process and works hand-in-hand with the patient as opposed to sitting back and only listening. CBT is designed to be a goal-oriented therapy where patients work with their therapists to achieve mutually determined goals. The individual is not kept in the dark about what CBT entails and is aware of all aspects of the therapeutic process.

The impact that CBT aims to make lies in the idea that thoughts and feelings play an underlying and fundamental role in one's behavior. For example, an individual who constantly thinks about car crashes searches for information about car accidents online and visualizes these incidents will most likely develop a fear of driving and avoid even taking a ride in a car. However, such an individual is not always aware that they have these thought patterns that border on obsession and even more so, that they cause certain negative or unrealistic reactions or behavior. This is where the effectiveness of CBT comes in. By firstly helping an individual to become aware of these persistent and influential thoughts paves the way to the next step, which is engaging with them and understanding them. For a child or teen with ODD, this process may be difficult, especially if they are still young, so the process of explaining it to them is crucial. The pros of CBT are that it has been empirically tested to work on individuals who demonstrate toxic behaviors, and it is usually a more affordable treatment option. Here are the CBT steps that lead to successful change and also two situations that can slow down or negatively impact the progress of CBT:

First, as we've discussed prior, is the identification of negative thoughts. First, the individual must understand how powerful their thoughts are and how their thoughts influence their emotions and behavior. If the individual who is undergoing CBT specifically struggles with introspection, they may need extra assistance as this is a key component to the identification of toxic thoughts and a new process of self-discovery.

Next, new skills that complement and enforce positive behavior need to be identified and implemented. The individual undergoing therapy will ultimately have to practice these skills in real-life situations that will start as a rehearsal process and eventually create a new neural pathway that will cause a natural tendency toward coping mechanisms and healthy behavior.

Along with the implementation of these new skills and coping mechanisms comes the setting of goals. Without setting goals, these positive reinforcement behaviors will move forward but have no destination.

It is also a crucial component of CBT to focus on the development of problem-solving skills. Problem-solving is part of critical thinking, and this skill will benefit your child even from a young age. Although they will not be able to identify all problems as objectivity is hard as a youngster, you can, with the support of the therapist, help them to systematically develop this life-changing skill. Teenagers will not have such a hard time developing problem-solving skills, although they may need a nudge in the right direction.

After taking all of this in, keep in mind that this transformation is going to be a gradual, if not slow, process. Rushing your child or teen to mentally transform may have the opposite effect, and you can, instead, give them a reason to work hard toward reaching their goal. Tell them how much you love them.

Parent-Child Interaction Therapy

Parent-child interaction therapy, or PCIT, is a combination of behavioral therapy and play therapy that works well for younger children and their caregivers or parents. During this therapeutic process, the adult learns novel skills and techniques that can improve the way they cope with children who have behavioral problems or disorders, emotional issues, language disorders, mental health issues, or language issues. This type of therapy focuses more on the adult to teach and empower them towards developing coping mechanisms and improving their communication with a troubled child, which can involve physical and verbal exchanges.

PCIT is developed for a specific age range, which is from 2 years to 7 years, and if you compare it to the description of cognitive behavioral theory, we discussed prior, as a parent, you'll immediately be able to recognize why this may be one of the more appropriate choices for younger children. For example, CBT focuses on the patient and allows them to go through an introspective process that a youngster of 2–3 years will not be able to understand. With PCIT, on the other hand, the control is given to the parents, and they are trained in changing possible triggering behavior and interaction with their young children.

During the PCIT process, parents play with their children in one room while the therapist observes and subsequently coaches the parents from an adjacent room separated by a one-way mirror. During the play process, the therapist and parent communicate using an earphone device to ensure that the parent's responses are specifically tailored to the behavior the child shows during that activity. This also creates a very effective learning process, which would have been based on trial-and-error, but here this element is not significantly reduced due to the observations and leadership of the therapist. Some of the advice a therapist would typically provide a parent is to steer clear of negative language and to ignore negative behavior if it is otherwise harmless. To counter this aspect, they are encouraged to praise for any positive behaviors and show their enthusiasm in these cases. Other skills include reflecting the child's language back to them, which helps them with communication, improving the child's vocabulary by describing the child's activities clearly and audibly and imitating their good behavior to show approval.

PCIT is, in many ways, a relationship-building process taking place in a controlled environment where parents, who take the lead in this process, have the ability to acquire new skills while practicing relationship-building. Improving the relationship, you have with your troubled young child can lead to improved behavior, and this can improve family dynamics overall. Long-term practice of this therapy has shown increased confidence in the child, a reduced level of anger, resentment, and aggression, and it ultimately regulates healthy interaction between the parent and the child.

If you recognize any benefits in this description of parent-child interaction therapy that you think may benefit your situation, specifically related to the age of your child, you can locate a qualified therapist by looking for a licensed mental health service provider that holds a master's degree or higher, and that preferably has undergone additional training in PCIT. Additionally, it is imperative that you and your child are able to bond with the therapist and that a trusting relationship can be formed (Psychology Today, 2020).

Group Psychotherapy

Group psychotherapy usually involves one or sometimes more than one therapist that works with a group of patients. This type of therapy can be used on its own but is also commonly used in tandem with other types of individual therapy and psychiatric treatment. Groups can start small, meaning they can consist of three to five individuals, but larger groups of up to twelve individuals can also work, especially if the patients bond well. A psychotherapy group would typically meet twice a week, and a session can last one to two hours. Group therapy sessions can be either open or closed, which means that, in some cases, new members are allowed to join during the course of the therapy period. In other cases, patients sign up before the sessions start, and the group membership remains the same.

A typical session for children may include musical therapy, art therapy, and play therapy. The way the sessions are conducted depends on the goal the therapists want to achieve and the condition of the patients. Group psychotherapy for teenagers may involve more talking, sharing of experiences, but expressive activities like art and music therapy will not be excluded as options due to their therapeutic effects. Therapists have a lot of freedom as to how they want sessions to be conducted, and some sessions can be structured while others can be more spontaneous and free-form.

Group Psychotherapy is used for a myriad of mental conditions and disorders, but it always strives to have the same benefits for its members. One benefit of this type of therapy can offer your child or teen is that they will be among peers, as well as under the supervision of therapists. While therapists set the breeding ground for positive interaction, the group members can offer support and encouragement by seeing that their fellow members possibly have the same issues and struggles. This can help them to feel less isolated than, for example, at home where they are the only person experiencing these emotions and outbursts. This leads us to the next proof of group psychotherapy, which is that it gives your child or teen a safe space where they may feel they can say or express things that they cannot do in front of you, at school, or at home.

Don't take this personally as it usually means that they may have some toxic feelings they want to get rid of that they don't want to expose you to, and if they are provided an open and safe environment to do so, getting rid of these pent-up emotions can be done is a much healthier way. What happens in the group stays in the group. And, what's especially relevant for children or teens with ODD in a group setting, the therapist can pay close attention to how they interact with others and how they behave in a social setting, which is usually a problematic situation for children and teens with ODD. Therapists can monitor their behavior and provide valuable feedback.

Finally, another plus is that group therapy is normally a more affordable option than cognitive behavioral therapy, which can have a major role-playing effect in some households (Cherry, 2009).

Applied Behavior Analysis

Applied behavior analysis is one of the treatment options that are often used for aggressive behavior and a lack of impulse control. These are not specifically disorders in themselves, but they are present in, for example, autism spectrum disorder, conduct disorder, oppositional defiant disorder, and intermittent explosive disorder, most of which are co-operational disorders, which includes our focal point, ODD.

Impulsive and aggressive behavior is often seen as behaviors that reinforce themselves in different social contexts because they have the ability to provoke an instant reaction from their target. This is because, if aggression or impulsive behavior is focused on you, your immediate reaction will be to address it immediately, which means that you gave the person projecting that behavior the attention they wanted. And, of course, your natural reaction to aggressiveness or impulsivity aimed at you will be negative and defensive, which only fuels that reinforcement even more. This is one of the reasons why it is so difficult to change aggressive and impulsive behaviors in children and teens, and applied behavior analysis specifically focuses on analyzing and constructively approaching these behaviors, tackling them proactively.

An applied behavioral therapist or ABA therapist will generally follow a procedure with their patients if the behavioral issue has not been established. They will start by determining which behavior needs attention and requires change and then set goals or identify outcomes that are expected from the therapeutic process. Further, the ABA therapist will, according to the individual situation, decide which measures and techniques they will apply and also establish ways to measure progress and changes in a patient's behavior. Furthermore, the ABA therapist may teach the patient new skills or coping mechanisms, review progress, and ultimately decide whether further behavior modification is necessary in a specific case. As each case is unique, the duration of the therapy is dependent on the severity of the issue and the rate of improvement shown by the patient.

When it comes to treating aggression and impulse control through applied behavior analysis, ABA-trained therapists are aware of the attention-related payoff that children and teens with relevant disorders get from these behaviors, so they are trained to show no external reactions toward overt aggressive behavior directed at them. They also train caregivers and parents to do the same. For example, an ABA therapist will advise you to offer a response called neutral redirection as an alternative to punitive measures when being confronted with aggressive behavior.

Neutral redirection is specifically part of applied behavior analysis treating aggression and impulse control-related disorders, and it focuses on empowering the caregiver or authoritative figure to handle the disruptive and aggressive behavior in such a way that it will be eventually subdued. In extreme cases where a child with conduct disorder was to hit a caregiver, they are trained to not show any reaction — not even the slightest flinch. By doing this, they completely dismantle the child's attempt at getting the desired reaction. Neutral redirection teaches the parent, teacher, or caregiver to avoid any reaction and eye contact with the child or teen, which essentially sends the message that they refuse to acknowledge the aggressive or impulsive behavior. When being aggressively attacked, their only response should be to stay calm and guide the aggressive child or teen towards engaging in a more socially acceptable way. Then, only when the child or teen starts behaving in the way they are instructed to by the caregiver will they receive attention and direct acknowledgment. Sounds hard, doesn't it? Trying to adjust to indicating no acknowledgment or reaction whatsoever while being aggressively harassed or insulted by a child requires an immense amount of self-control.

However, looking at ABA and its approach from a more general perspective as it is used for more type's conditions than just aggression and impulsivity-related ones, it is important for an ABA therapist to understand how individuals learn certain human behaviors and, based on this principle, how it can be changed or altered over the course of time. The therapist starts by evaluating the child's or teen's behavior and develops a treatment plan based thereon to improve communication and behavioral aspects that need alteration for the child or teen's optimal functioning and development into adulthood. As demonstrated above, one of the pros of ABA therapy is that the therapist can train the caregiver, teacher, and adult. However, for this type of therapy to be effective, continuous evaluation and considerable measures should be taken for effective patient monitoring. As progression starts to show, treatment is modified to fit and promote further progression.

If you are looking for a qualified and able ABA therapist, their practice requirements include graduate-level to a doctorate-level degree; they need to be licensed as a clinical therapist and have additional training and experience in ABA (Psychology Today, 2016; AppliedBehaviorAnalysisEdu.org, 2020).

Family Therapy

Family therapy is classified as a specific type of psychotherapy that traditionally requires the involvement of all members of a nuclear family or a stepfamily, and in some cases, it can also involve members of the extended family, depending on their relevance to the situation. The family members attend sessions together that are conducted by either one therapist or a team of therapists who aim to help the family deal or work through issues that are causing dysfunctionalities in the family dynamics and home environment.

The purpose of family therapy is specifically to improve family dynamics, even if there is only one member in the family who has a problem or suffers from an illness. Some of the reasons families attend therapy sessions together are because of the loss of a family member, a mental or physical illness, or issues involving children or teens like ODD. In a case like this or any other case where family therapy is used to deal with the disorder of a child or teen, the purpose is mostly to work through what causes the family's inability to function normally and, similarly, when a new stepfamily has come together and new family dynamics are in the process of forming. At the beginning of the 21st century, therapists started applying a new approach called multisystemic therapy or MST, which is most often done at the family's home so the therapist can experience the ecological environment of the family they are treating. MST is thus often called the "family-ecological systems approach" because a therapist looks at how a family interacts within their home environment. This approach is used especially when there is a problem child or teen with behavioral issues or emotional disturbances. Several clinical research studies have been conducted on MST, and the general consensus is that it improves family relations, can decrease adolescent substance use and psychiatric symptoms, and can improve school attendance.

Family therapy can be conducted by counselors, therapists, social workers, or psychiatrists and involve multiple sessions over an extended period of time. For example, a session would mostly last one hour, and these sessions can occur once a week for three or four months. Here are some interesting concepts related to family therapy, specifically:

The Identified Patient: The identified patient or IP is the individual in the family that is the reason for the family attending family therapy. This makes it sound like we're placing the blame on the IP, but we're simply stating that because of this individual experiencing specific issues or being diagnosed with a specific disorder like ODD, this type of therapy is required and thus attended.

Homeostasis: Homeostasis is a Greek word that means 'balance,' and this word refers to the situation or goal the family seeks to achieve through family therapy. The family wants to restore or work on any situations or causal factors that are causing an imbalance in family dynamics, and thereby reinstate homeostasis or harmonious family life and relationships.

The Extended Family Field: This term is used to describe the immediate family, the network of grandparents, and also includes other family members. In other words, not only the nuclear family. The extended family field is also a term used to refer to and identify what is called an intergenerational transmission of behaviors, problems, and attitudes or emotions. Including members of the extended family, the field can benefit from family therapy that is specifically centered around a child or teen.

Differentiation: This term describes each individual family member's ability to be their own person but, at the same time, be able to integrate into a familial community and be part of a greater whole, which is the family. Thus, a healthy family is one that allows differentiation among its members and accepts them as individuals.

Triangular Relationships: This is an interesting family relationship theory that is also often observed in family therapy. The theory says that, when a troubled situation develops between two family members, they are likely to draw in a third member to stabilize the situation and maintain homeostasis. Some examples of a typical triangular relationship are two parents and a child, a parent, a child, and a grandparent, three children, or two children and a parent. These triangles occur as a natural way to maintain homeostasis in a family setting.

For effective family therapy, a family therapist will first schedule appointments with family members to conduct a series of interviews. These interviews always include all members of the nuclear or stepfamily, but other members can also be interviewed for relevant purposes. For example, if there is an extended family member with a psychiatric illness, the therapist may want to interview this individual, which can help them understand if there are other indirect contributing factors. The interviews allow each family member to provide their version of the issue, and the therapist can get a first impression from each member individually and how they contribute to the functioning of the family before the group sessions start.

Things therapists look for in these interviews include the type and levels of emotions expressed by the individual, signs of dominance or submission, the role played by every member in the family, how different members communicate, and whether there are any obvious relationship triangles. The therapist then draws a genogram as part of the preparation process. A genogram is a type of diagram that shows significant events and persons in the family's history and can contain medical history and information on major personality traits. With a genogram, the therapist is able to identify behavioral patterns that stretch over more than one generation, typical marriage choices, possible family secrets, family alliances and previous situations of conflict, and any other details that may be useful for the specific family the therapist is focusing on.

As a final thought regarding family therapy, as effective as it may be on its own and in conjunction with other types of therapy, there are situations in which one needs to take precautions and think about whether the nature of this therapy is suitable for the situation you are experiencing. Examples include families where one or both parents suffer from mental illnesses that include psychosis, antisocial tendencies, or paranoia. Another example is if a family's inherent cultural or religious values do not recognize psychotherapy or harbors suspicions of its practices. A more common example would be a family that is not physically able to meet regularly enough for effective therapy to be conducted. It's always best to look at the pros and cons, but family therapy, and especially MST, is a great option for children and teens with ODD that causes disruption in a household (Encyclopedia of Children's Health, 2020).

Psychological Counseling for Children and Adolescents

A child psychologist is specifically trained to help a child understand themselves from their own perspective. In other words, if a child has a disorder or a mental illness, the psychologist will help them to figure out what's going on in their minds by using their way of thinking and reasoning as a starting point. Child counseling focuses on children, adolescents, and teens that battle with mental disorders or mental illnesses. Additionally, this type of counseling is used to help children who are experiencing trauma or high levels of grief, or who live in a dysfunctional environment at home. The goal of child counseling is to break down stressful situations and problems children experience to make them seem more approachable and, ultimately, conquerable. If your child is someone who is trained to see things and communicate things to them from their level and perspective, then child counseling can greatly benefit your child or teenager.

Because child counselors are trained to communicate with your child or teenager on their level instead of trying to lift them to your level, the child may bond more easily with the counselor, a trusting relationship can be established quicker, and your child is likely to tell the counselor things about their life and their feelings that are important and relevant to their condition, but that they would never have revealed under other circumstances.

Child counselors are trained to treat a wide variety of issues that children and teenagers experience. These issues include disorders and mental illness, but also expand to grief and trauma like divorce, relocation, the death of a loved one, bullying, sexual or emotional abuse, and family-related addiction or substance abuse. They also tend to use methods like cognitive behavioral therapy if they think it is the best way to treat a child's condition, but their approach would differ slightly because of their specialized training. From a child counselor's perspective, there are specific behavioral signs that can be an indicator that your child or teen can benefit from child counseling. These include the leakage of urine, unprovoked aggression if the child has significant difficulty adjusting to new situations like a social situation, issues with academic performance if your child experiences constant and excessive anxiety, a sudden disinterest in previous hobbies and activities, addiction or drug abuse, self-harm, or hearing voices.

If you feel that your child needs this specific approach, then you can try a child counselor to see if your child benefits from this specialized method of communication (Langham, 2019).

Psychiatry

Drug treatment for ODD is not deemed as the first best option as there are no FDA-approved medications for oppositional defiant disorder in the United States. This being said, there are specific drugs that can perform a "rewiring" process in the brain and improve the symptoms of ODD in children and adolescents. Children diagnosed with ODD have shown signs of improved behavior when administered low doses of atypical neuroleptics like Abilify (aripiprazole) and Risperdal (risperidone). Medication should, however, not be considered a primary option due to the absence of approved medicative substances (Rodden, 2017).

Homeopathy

There are individuals who believe that ODD can be treated with homeopathic remedies, and there are many individuals who are opposed to psychiatric medicine due to its many side effects. Homeopathy is used for ODD but is a lesser-known treatment option. Let's look at what homeopathy entails and how homeopathic treatments can work for your ODD child or teen and which ones are recommended.

Homeopathy is classified as a medical science that, in its diagnostic process, considers the physiological and psychological components of an individual in relation to how the disease in question has evolved in the body or mind. This concept is used and all these factors are considered when prescribing a homeopathic remedy. A homeopath believes that by using this method, they are more likely to find the root cause of an illness or a disorder as a medical doctor only looks at the physical and a psychiatrist focuses on pharmaceutical drugs, while their remedies remain natural. Considering these details, it is safe to say that homeopathy has a holistic methodology.

When consulting a homeopath, they will take down a record of your physical ailments, including undiagnosed complaints, physical and psychological attributes, and the emotional situation you are in during the consultation. This approach makes it easier for the practitioner to find the root cause of an issue by looking at it through a holistic lens, and it gives the patient the opportunity to rid themselves of any thoughts that have been bothering them, as these thoughts will also be deemed important by the homeopath.

As opposed to psychiatric medicine, homeopathic remedies are deemed to be safe, they have no side effects, and they are in their natural form. Homeopathic remedies are also known to improve the immune system and renew energy levels. Homeopathic medicine aims to balance the psychological, biological, and emotional issues or disturbances a child experiences when they have ODD and subsequently improves the child's behavior. Homeopathic medicine also claims to prevent an ODD child from experiencing a relapse, which would be a recurrent episode that happens after the child started the treatment. By using homeopathic medicine, the child's mind, which is in distress, can be stabilized and positive behavior can start developing. An interesting trait of homeopathic medicine is that it is patient-oriented, which means that the medicine prescribed is based on the characteristics of the patient instead of solely on the symptoms of the condition. As you will see, the recommended medicines include characteristics that are not part of ODD's usual symptoms. Here are three examples:

- CINA: This remedy is especially effective for children who are irritable, anxious, and restless. The child can also be described as petulant, dissatisfied, angry, and dislikes to be touched. The child is very demanding but will not accept anything that is offered to him. These children also tend to be overweight and have a large appetite.

- NATRUM MURIATICUM: Treatment for children who are irritable, easily offended, impulsive, and can be abusive towards others. This remedy can also help if a child is malnourished or needs vitamins.

- ANTIMONIUM CRUDUM: This remedy is specifically for children who have excessive anger and act in an abusive way towards others. The child is moody, will often ignore someone who speaks to them, and can easily become irritated. They seem to get angry for no reason and they crave attention (Welcome Cure, 2020).

As you can see, these remedies are extremely specific and sometimes contain strange information about the person its treatment is aimed at. However, there are more than 50 different remedies used to treat Oppositional Defiant Disorder in homeopathy, whereas in psychiatric medicine there are two. The question is, will your child fit the profile of one of those fifty remedies? It is an interesting methodology, and the experience may be therapeutic for the soul.

ODD Home Care

One of the most difficult challenges of living with an ODD child or teen is to separate their violent and disruptive behavior from who they are as a person because they are not their disorder. They are children/young adults that require direction and affection. Because you usually associate people with the way they behave, to suddenly not do it is incredibly difficult, especially if it is your own flesh and blood. Here are a few tips that can help you to manage and stabilize an otherwise stormy household.

Firstly, don't react to or engage in a power struggle with your child or teen. If you are an ODD mom, you know that this is something they instigate often, and you can dismantle the potential conflict situation just as quickly by not going for the bait. Another way to keep a steady boat is to choose which battles you want to fight and which you'll leave. For example, there will be lots of provocation and opportunistic attempts at conflict, but some will be more serious than others. Do you have to react to a provocation if it's not that serious? The idea of not reacting doesn't mean you should always ignore your child, but you can respond in a non-confrontational way which shows them that you are willing to pay attention, but you are not available for fighting about willy-nilly stuff.

Then, you know they're going to break them, but it's imperative to establish and uphold clear rules in the household and make it clear that it is unacceptable when a rule is broken. An ODD child or teen is going to use this structure to rebel against, but without a clear household structure, you are not providing the child with a good example of how to live their life. This being said, you should also provide your child with the opportunity to express themselves in the form of innocent play. These are moments of healthy expression, so enjoy them with your child or teen if you can.

Try not to bombard your child or teen with too many questions, even if you have some burning ones. If they look like they want to talk, then they are showing you a need to talk, but you have this handy little guide for any general information about ODD you may need. Don't depend on or expect your child to explain the disorder to you as this can be burdensome for them.

Help your child to follow a routine as this structure can be something they can lean on when things don't go well. This may sound strange as ODD children and teens seem to want to destroy routine and authority, but you can find a way to suggest it to them that will have them slip into it without them even noticing. Routine for someone with a mental or mood disorder can be like a walking frame when every limb in their body feels like it doesn't want to move. Finding a way to introduce a sense of routine without appearing authoritative, which can spark a reaction or an episode, is the trick (Mauro, 2019).

Chapter 10. ADHD and ODD

Sometimes, a child might be displaying defiance not just because of ODD, but because they also have ADHD, which might turn out to be the primary cause of their challenging behavior.

How can two disorders occur together? And how can you identify if your child has both? Let's take a look.

The Difference Between ODD and ADHD

You now know a relative amount about the oppositional defiant disorder, but many kids who exhibit some extreme form of troublesome behavior might have a co-occurring disorder as well. Several children with ODD also have ADHD, even though not every child with attention deficit hyperactivity disorder is diagnosed with the oppositional defiant disorder.

Irrespective of the fact that there is no medical treatment for ODD, a child with both disorders will benefit from behavioral modification practices as well as medication to improve their symptoms.

When your child exhibits signs linked to ODD, your clinician might recommend a comprehensive mental evaluation. Once ODD has been diagnosed and there might be indications of ADHD as well, your doctor might advise a test period where your child will have to take ADHD medication to treat this particular disorder, which could actually improve ODD symptoms.

Hot Blooded or Frustrated?

A child who suffers from ADHD can become annoyed because they struggle to deal with their frustrations or educational obstacles. It might seem like an expression of anger or insolence. Kids with ODD, throw temper tantrums because they are being deprived of something they want. Their behavior is completely deliberate, whereas a child with ADHD did not pre-contemplate their actions.

Impulsive or Aggressive?

As mentioned, kids with ADHD "do first and think second." They are habitually impulsive and generally, these kids are not intentionally spiteful. Kids with ODD act out on purpose. A child with ADHD might push their classmate down the slide because they want to slide too, a child with ODD will push a kid down the slide because the child is in their way. If the classmate gets hurt, your kid with ADHD will feel terrible because of their actions; an ODD kid will feel they won the battle.

Inattentiveness or Defiance?

With both disorders, parents will give instructions and children will not listen to them. The behavior is identical, but the reasons behind the behaviors vary. An ODD child acts defiantly on purpose because they do not want to adhere to any authority figure's rules. They intentionally refuse to cooperate. A child with ADHD hears you, but is completely distracted, and forgets very quickly what was said if they are interested in something else. It is not deliberate disobedience.

Struggles with Relationships

Both disorders cause isolation and issues with friendships. A child with ADHD struggles to make friends because they misunderstand people. They interrupt people and speak without thinking, which could upset their peers accidentally. They are socially uncomfortable. Kids with ODD push people away on purpose. They enjoy hurting others emotionally and physically. They will cause fights and arguments intentionally and lie without a conscience.

What are the Symptoms of ADHD and ODD?

Behaviorally signs and symptoms of ADHD and ODD can appear identical, but the child's motives are totally unrelated. Luckily, many kids with ODD will outgrow these qualities before they reach adolescence. Medications will help for ADHD and by dealing with symptoms such as depression signs of ODD could also diminish. Then again, these disorders might progress into conduct disorders that might last during adolescence or even when they become fully mature. Any healthcare provider should pay careful attention to all signs, symptoms, and reasons for both ODD as well as ADHD disorders before making a final diagnosis.

If you noticed that your child's behaviors are more spiteful or deliberate instead of emotional or impulsive, you need to go and consult your local GP for a referral to a mental health/behavioral expert.

If your child's mental and behavioral activities show indications of both conditions, it is possible that these ailments are running concurrently. Signs and symptoms for both disorders must exist for a minimum of six months before a proper diagnosis can be made.

Indications of ODD

- Blame shifting

- Quickly annoyed and offended

- Resentment towards authority figures

- Refuses to obey rules

- Loss of temper or aggravated easily

- Deliberately irritates or shocks others

- Malicious and Spiteful

ADHD Indicators

- Trouble with concentration

- Continuous fiddling

- Intruding in discussions

- Easily confused and disordered

- Unfocused

- Often losing items

- Incapable of taking notes at school

- Fails to recall daily school projects or other responsibilities

- Excessive talking

- Blurting out responses

- Difficulty heeding and following instructions

What are the Origins of ADHD and ODD?

The initial source of these disorders remains unidentified, but we do know genetics and environmental impacts are some of the main reasons for developing them. There are various symptoms of hereditary disorders and could contain types of behavior that bring about self-mutilation or physical harm. Other symptoms include hostility and difficulty with impulse control.

Environmental influences also play a huge role in both disorders and immense, continuous exposure to physical tyranny, negligence or corporal punishment is the main causes of these conditions.

Children with ODD might outgrow many of the characteristics and a rebellious adolescent could become an easy-going adult. Still, other behavioral complications such as hostility might turn into an enduring struggle.

ODD and ADHD Diagnosis

Diagnostically, there is no particular evaluation to identify ADHD or ODD. A psychological, as well as a medical checkup, is required to dismiss all other probable causes such as depression or an educational debility before a proper diagnosis can be made. A child can have both disorders but only display a few symptoms, so an expert will need to examine their family and personal past, as well as consult with educators, childminders, or other individuals they interact with on a regular basis. It's critical that you find out the treatment options your doctor recommends.

Treatments Options

A dual diagnosis such as ODD and ADHD usually requires both medical and therapeutic treatment approaches. Medications will ease physical and mental symptoms such as restlessness and inattentiveness, whereas counseling and therapy will assist with moderating defiant behaviors. Other treatment options include family therapy combined with social skills training to improve communication between parents and kids. Cognitive problem-solving skills that aid in correcting adverse thought patterns, as well as social skills training methods to acquire the appropriate skills to relate to others. Sometimes ODD children can be a danger to themselves or the community and hospitalization might be required, which can be involuntary for a period of 72 hours for medical observation if necessary.

The Connection Between ODD and ADHD

According to Attitudemag.com, nearly 40% of kids who suffer from ADHD are diagnosed with ODD as well. Specialists believe that ODD can be linked to the lack of impulse control associated with ADHD, while kids with ADHD display oppositional features connected to ODD, even though their defiant behaviors are not deliberate. The same article also proposed that ODD is a type of coping mechanism for feelings of frustration and emotional hurt related to their ADHD.

ADHD and ODD Treatment Options

- Your child's ADHD symptoms can be regulated with the correct medications.

- Behavioral modification methods will ensure an improved demeanor.

- Children with extreme behavioral and mental issues will need to see a qualified family therapist and undergo a full-on psychological screening for any other disorders like anxiety, bipolar, and depression.

Conclusion

Odds are you have never heard of this disorder, or if you have, it was probably through a news article. It is a moderately uncommon type of oppositional defiant disorder (ODD) where the child will exhibit an unusually high degree of defiance and anger against authority figures (i.e., parents and teachers) while simultaneously engaging in low levels of compliance with those same authority figures. However, while ODD is a list of symptoms that are characterized by the child's characteristic passive-aggressive defiance and rebelliousness, it is quite different from a typical case of ODD.

In particular, the circumstances surrounding these children's defiant behavior often appear to be circumstantial; for example, an argument with the parent that leads to the child becoming angry. If this anger does not lead to an outburst or action such as hitting or breaking something or falling down in front of others, then it may not meet the criteria for the oppositional defiant disorder (ODD). As such, the child in question may be experiencing atypical cases of ODD, or may even be experiencing some form of bipolar disorder.

Although the concept of oppositional defiant disorder (ODD) has been around for many years, it is not very well recognized by physicians or psychologists. However, we have observed children exhibiting some unusual behaviors that indicate this possibility and have also seen children who fit the oppositional defiant behavior pattern but do not fit the criteria for ODD. As such, we have devised a list of symptoms that are indicative of ODD that cannot be attributed to another condition and that can be distinguished from typical childhood defiance and rebellion. These symptoms are:

1. The child is consolable (the child is capable of calming down after an episode of defiance and becoming complacent)
2. The child does not engage in outbursts directed towards self or others (i.e., the child does not lash out when defiant but remains calm)
3. The defiance is not limited to just one area but is exhibited in all areas (such as tantrums, anger, rigidity, and belligerence)
4. The defiant behavior occurs only with adults and never with peers

Interestingly enough, we have also observed children who appear to have a case of bipolar disorder but who exhibit some of these same symptoms suggestive of oppositional defiant disorder. The typical symptoms of bipolar disorder are:

1. The child exhibits manic or hypomanic episodes (i.e., a peak of euphoria, increased energy, and a heightened sense of self-importance)
2. These episodes are also common times when the child exhibits defiance and anger towards authority figures (including parents and teachers)
3. This defiance is limited to just one area — what the child wants versus what others around them want
4. The defiance and anger are not consolable

The best way to differentiate between bipolar disorder and oppositional defiant disorder is to create a "profile" of the child that includes their mood, behavior, and activity level throughout the past several weeks. It is unlikely that you have bipolar disorder if these symptoms remain for an extended period of time with no apparent changes in mood, activity level, or behavior. Similarly, if there is any other day where the child is extremely upset but then calms down relatively quickly and returns to normal with no other days above baseline (i.e., typical), then this is lined up with bipolar but not ODD.

It's also worth noting that youngsters who have been depressed may develop megalomania, in which they believe they can do no wrong and are always correct. In these children, it is usually the parents and teachers who are seen as the outside source of authority. The child with oppositional defiant behavior may also have a sense of entitlement to their demands (i.e., make all the decisions, be bossing everyone around, etc.).

Thank you for getting this far. I have spent so much time writing this manuscript, and now I kindly ask you to help me with the popularization. This would mean so much to me; it would really give me immense pleasure to receive a positive review from you on Amazon; your reviews are much more important than you know!